MW01177905

So OFTEN, as new Christians, we labor under the mistaken impression that once we have accepted Jesus into our lives everything should go smoothly from then on. When we run into some rough spots (and we all do!) we often discover our newfound faith shaken.

This is what was happening to the new believers in Thessalonica. They were living in the midst of a pagan culture with temptations all around them. Their faith was threatened at every turn, they faced hostility from the many unbelievers living around them, and confusing rumors abounded concerning the second coming of Christ.

Sound familiar? In studying Paul's letters to the Thessalonians you will be encouraged in your Christian walk to hang on, to press on, and to keep on growing!

**Other good Regal Reading in the
Bible Commentary for Laymen Series:**

Confronted by Love (2 Corinthians)
by Dan Baumann

You Are Loved and Forgiven (Colossians)
by Lloyd John Ogilvie

Winning the Battles of Life (Joshua)
by Paul E. Toms

How to Live What You Believe (Hebrews)
by Ray C. Stedman

LET'S KEEP GROWING!

ENCOURAGEMENT FROM 1ST AND 2ND THESSALONIANS

HAROLD L. FICKETT

GL
Regal Books
A Division of GL Publications
Ventura, California, U.S.A.

Published by Regal Books
A Division of GL Publications
Ventura, California 93006
Printed in U.S.A.

Scripture taken from the HOLY BIBLE: NEW INTERNATIONAL VERSION.
Copyright © 1973, 1978, 1984 by the International Bible Society. Used by permission of Zondervan Bible Publishers.

Also used are:

KJV-King James Version
TLB—*The Living Bible,* Copyright © 1971 by Tyndale House Publishers, Wheaton, Illinois. Used by permission.

© Copyright 1977,1987 by Regal Books
All rights reserved.

Originally published under the title *Keep on Keeping On.*

Library of Congress Cataloging-in-Publication Data

Fickett, Harold L.
    Let's keep growing!

    1. Bible. N.T. Thessalonians—Criticism, interpretation, etc.   I. Title.
BS2725.2.F53   1987   227'.8107   87-4822
ISBN 0-8307-1192-9 (pbk.)

3 4 5 6 7 8 9 10

Rights for publishing this book in other languages are contracted by Gospel Literature International (GLINT) foundation. GLINT also provides technical help for the adaptation, translation, and publishing of Bible study resources and books in scores of languages worldwide. For further information, contact GLINT, Post Office Box 488, Rosemead, California, 91770, U.S.A., or the publisher.

Any omission of credits or permissions granted is unintentional. The publisher requests documentation for future printings.

Contents

Introduction to
1 and 2 Thessalonians

God's ways are not always man's ways. Numerous illustrations of this axiom are found in the history of Christianity. A case in point is that of Paul's taking the gospel to Europe. Had he followed his own desire he would have gone into northern Asia. But God had other plans. Paul had a vision which he took as God's direction to go to Macedonia (see Acts 16:6-10).

So Paul went to Macedonia, and ministered in the three strategic centers in that area—Philippi, Thessalonica, and Berea—for each of these had large Jewish communities.

The story of Paul's visit to Thessalonica is recorded in Acts 17:1-10. Even though his stay there was probably no more than three to four weeks (see Acts 17:2), his efforts were crowned with success. Many people turned to Christ as Saviour and Lord; the Thessalonian church was organized and, despite the opposition from the pagan culture around them, the members of this church continued the ministry for the Saviour in their city. Both 1 and 2 Thessalonians were addressed to them.

Naturally Paul was concerned about the well-being of this infant church. After leaving the area, he sent Timothy back to Thessalonica to investigate what was taking place there. The news that Timothy brought back was most encouraging and heart warming.

Paul's response was to write the church a letter of encouragement and praise. In essence he told them, "You're doing well; keep it up!" (see 1 Thess. 4:1).

All was not sweetness and light, however. Along with the encouraging news there were some disturbing facts brought to light. Basically these were four:

First, Paul's opponents in Thessalonica had started a whispering campaign against him in which they sought to undermine his character (see 1 Thess. 2:5-7,9,11).

Second, there were those who had lost their Christian loved ones and were concerned about their future well-being (see 1 Thess. 4:13-18).

Third, there was the ever-present threat that some of the church members would relapse into their old pagan ways of doing things (see 1 Thess. 4:3-8).

Fourth, there was the hint that a division might develop in the church (see 1 Thess. 4:9; 5:13).

The purpose of Paul's writing 1 Thessalonians was threefold: to commend them for the good things which Timothy reported; to answer questions which were disturbing them; and to admonish them to correct the evil trends which were apparently developing.

Evangelical scholarship is pretty well agreed that 1 Thessalonians was the first of Paul's New Testament letters to be written. And it is agreed that the date of its writing was somewhere between A.D. 50 and A.D. 54, and that Corinth was the place where it was written.

The question now arises "Why 2 Thessalonians?"

Even cursory reading of this epistle reveals that there were two reasons for it.

First, 2 Thessalonians 2:1-12 makes it clear that someone had written a letter to the church claiming it was from Paul and stating that the "day of the Lord" had already come. The rapture had taken place, and they had missed it. Naturally, they were greatly disturbed by this. Paul corrected this false impression by disclaiming his authorship of the disturbing letter (see 2 Thess. 2:2), and declaring that the "day of the Lord" was still in the future.

Second, there were some members of the church who felt that they should quit their jobs, let someone else support them, and sit down and wait for the Lord's return. Paul corrected this in chapter 3.

There is general agreement among evangelical scholars that this second epistle was written shortly after Paul received the response of the Thessalonians to his first epistle. In all probability this was brought to him by the bearer of the first epistle. This means that 2 Thessalonians likely was written while Paul was still in Corinth on his second missionary journey. While it is difficult to pinpoint the exact date of the writing, in all probability it was among the first of his New Testament writings. Many scholars list 2 Thessalonians as the second epistle which Paul wrote. Its writing is placed in Corinth about A.D. 51.

1
You Can Be a Model Christian

1 Thessalonians 1:1-10

In writing 1 Thessalonians, Paul established a pattern which he emulated in six of the other New Testament books which came from his inspired pen. Simply stated, it is the pattern of immediately following the salutation with an expression of thanksgiving.

Notice the way this pattern works out in verses 1 and 2. In verse 1 he wrote "Paul, Silas and Timothy, To the church of the Thessalonians in God the Father and the Lord Jesus Christ: Grace and peace to you." In this salutation he called attention to the fact that he was the author of the book; that his collaborators were Silas and Timothy; and that grace and peace were extended to the recipients of the letter.

Grace and peace are available to every living person. Grace is the provision of eternal life through the death and resurrection of Jesus Christ which Almighty God offers as a gift to every individual. Peace—internal, sweet peace—is the inevitable result in the life of the person who by faith accepts that gift.

We Give Thanks

Immediately following the salutation comes an expression of gratitude in verse 2: "We always thank God for all of you, mentioning you in our prayers."

In establishing the pattern of the greeting first, followed immediately by an expression of thanks, Paul demonstrated his profound knowledge of the human psyche. He knew that people needed encouragement and that once this has been given them they will listen without resentment to any corrective suggestion which is offered. In this book Paul dealt with the problems of the people in no uncertain terms; but he softened the blow by expressing gratitude to them for the good things they had done.

From time to time this is what we all need. Husbands would do well to remember this in their relationship to their wives. When a wife knocks herself out to do something special for her family, the smart husband will heap praises on her for it.

Wives, too, have their responsibilities at this point. Contrary to what they may think, husbands appreciate being thanked for all they do. They are human beings. They need to be encouraged. Wise is the wife who not only realizes this, but does something about it.

Children, because they are related to their parents, are in the same boat. Certainly Paul had this in mind when he wrote in Ephesians 6:4: "Fathers, do not exasperate your children"—don't always ride them for the wrong things they do, while ignoring the many good things they accomplish.

When I was growing up my dad called me "Doc." I can remember his saying things like, "Doc, that's great"; "Doc, you did a fine thing there." Every time he said something like this it made me feel warm and good on the inside; it motivated me to want to please him all the more.

As we examine Paul's thanksgiving for the church in Thessalonica, we discover that it is threefold: "We continually remember before our God and Father your work produced by faith, your labor prompted by love, and your endurance inspired by hope in our Lord Jesus Christ" (1 Thess. 1:3).

Work of Faith

First, Paul—and God, who inspired him to write this letter—were grateful for their work of faith. The Lord does not choose to reveal to us exactly what that work was. But there are two things that He does reveal: it was a work of faith, and He was grateful for it. God is always pleased and grateful for any work of faith that glorifies Christ, regardless of how great or small the work may be.

This is a difficult concept for many people to grasp. They have the idea that unless they can do something gigantic for God, thereby demonstrating that they have great faith, they might as well forget it. Anything small is of such little consequence that the Lord pays no attention to it.

Don't you believe this! It is the devil's lie. Any work of faith, regardless of size, is of tremendous consequence in the sight of our Saviour.

Let me give you a case in point. Do you remember the widow described in Mark 12:41-44? By faith she brought to the Temple treasury two mites worth about a cent or a little less. Measured by the standard of size this was not much of a gift; and yet Jesus had far more to say about her than about all the others who were casting in large sums of money. You ask why? Because it took great faith for her to do what she did; those two mites were all she had. And the Lord was truly grateful for her work of faith.

A number of years ago I called on a woman who was bedfast because of a severe heart attack. As we talked, she said in effect, "I am so discouraged that I can hardly stand myself. I used to be so active for the Lord. But now I have been laid aside by this illness, and I can't do anything. Oh, how I wish that once again I could work for the Saviour."

Very quietly I looked at her and then in a subdued voice, I said, "Mrs. M, you can. As a matter of fact, you are in a position now to have the greatest ministry for God that you have ever had. You have time on your hands; you have no place to go. You can use your time in praying for God's servants all over the world. Begin by remembering me as your pastor before the throne of God, and then pray for all of the Christian workers whom you know."

Tears came to her eyes as she responded, "Why hadn't I thought of that? I will begin immediately." And she did. Every time I visited her, she spent time telling me about the various ministers and missionaries for whom she had been praying. You talk about a happy woman, she was surely that. I am sure that when she departed this life and went to be with the Lord, the first thing He did was to thank her for her work of faith. Will you have a similar experience when you see Him face to face?

Labor of Love

Second, Paul was thankful for the believers' labor of love. Living in the midst of a city which, for the most part, was hostile to them, they maintained a consistent ministry of love in which they sought to meet the needs of those about them with the help of and through the power of the Holy Spirit.

Today Christians all over the world are responding in the same way to the needs of man, and God is thankful for it. In the case of some, their labor of love is almost indescribable.

Ruby and Dick, a young couple in our church who are both blind, lead our program for the blind.

In a staff meeting Ruby shared with us the story of a 29-year-old mother whose husband deserted her when she lost her eyesight. One night she sat by the bedside of her 18-month-old child with a butcher knife in her hand. You can well imagine the thought that must have coursed through her mind. But the Lord was merciful and kept her and the child from tragedy.

Ruby met the young woman and began witnessing to her, in love, how Jesus Christ could meet her need. Finally, after about nine months, she invited the Saviour into her life. As Ruby told this, tears of joy streamed down her cheeks.

And there is a sequel to that story. The young woman has moved to another part of California. In her new area she has started a labor of love by interesting her new church in starting a program for the blind. Even though she is greatly limited—she cannot even read Braille because diabetes has destroyed the sensitivity of her fingertips—she is serving the Lord. And it all came about because another blind woman was engaged in a labor of love. Don't you know that our Saviour is grateful for both of these women? Is He grateful for you because of your labor of love?

Steadfast Hope

Third, Paul was grateful for the steadfastness of the believers' hope in our Lord Jesus Christ. These people bought the idea that the ultimate answer to every problem they faced was in Jesus Christ; this was their hope, their confidence, their assurance. It enabled them steadfastly to endure whatever came their way—whether it was persecution, privation, or even death itself.

Several years ago while on a preaching mission in Manila, I met a most unusual woman whose name is Olga Robertson. For more than 20 years she has worked at the New Bilibib prison as a chaplain. She has so won the confidence of the administration of that institution that they require every man on death row to have at least an hour's interview with her. She has been instrumental in winning hundreds of those men to Christ just before they were executed.

She told me about one of these men. About an hour and a half before he was strapped into the chair, he invited Christ into his life. As they took him into the execution chamber, she was permitted to go with him and stand where she could look him in the eye. Neither was allowed to speak to the other. Just before the switch was pulled, she formed on her lips the word, "Christo"; he responded by doing the same. The execution order was then given and he went out to meet face to face the Christ whom he had met by faith just a few minutes before. You talk about hope, confidence, assurance!

You Are Elected

Paul presented an amazing fact as he wrote "Brothers loved by God, we know that he has chosen you" (1 Thess. 1:4). The word "chosen" means "election." "We know" means "we see." In effect, Paul was saying, "We know your election on the basis of what we have seen."

What did Paul mean by this? He was pointing out that

on the basis of what he had seen in Thessalonica in the lives of the people, all who professed to be Christians in that church were exactly that. They were free from hypocrisy. They had had a genuine born-again experience.

Now it seems to me I can hear someone saying, "I can't imagine a church where all of the members are genuine Christians. I don't see in verse 4 all that you are saying. How do you know that your interpretation is correct?"

The answer is twofold: first, because of Paul's use of the phrase, "Brothers loved by God," and second, because of his use of the word "election" in referring to them.

Brothers Loved by God

Originally the phrase, "Brothers loved by God," was used by the Jews to describe the great men of the Old Testament—men about whom there was no doubt as to the favor which they enjoyed in God's eyes. In applying it to the Thessalonian Christians, Paul was saying, "You have the same standing in God's eyes as the great patriarchs of the Old Testament. You, like they, are truly children of the Almighty."

And what Paul taught here about the New Testament Christians of Thessalonica is true of every one of us who has sincerely surrendered his life to Jesus Christ as Saviour and Lord. We are just as valuable in God's sight, we are just as precious to the Almighty, as the great personalities of the Scriptures.

Through Paul's use of the word "election" in referring to the Thessalonian believers, we are brought face to face with the one doctrine in the Bible, the doctrine of election, which I believe has been more abused than any other New Testament teaching.

There are those, for example, who teach that God has elected or predestined some to be saved and elected and predestined others to be lost. The individual has no choice in the matter; he is simply at the mercy of a fatalistic course of action that has been predetermined for him by an Omnipotent God.

Throughout the Scripture this teaching is refuted. For example, Paul wrote in Romans 10:13, "For, 'Everyone who calls on the name of the Lord will be saved.'" Basic to this statement and that which gives it meaning is the fact that man has been created as a free moral agent with a will of his own; he can use that will to accept or reject Christ; he is not merely a puppet on a string. He is a person, created in the image of God.

In 1 Timothy 2:4 Paul said that God "wants all men to be saved and to come to a knowledge of the truth." It is God's will that every man be saved by coming into the experiential knowledge of the truth. If a person is not saved, God is not to be blamed; the fault lies with the man himself because he has exercised his will against, rather than for, the Lord Jesus Christ.

The best explanation of election I have ever heard is the simplest; it was given by a southern country preacher. He said, "God votes for you; the devil votes against you; and whichever way you vote, you are elected."

The Thessalonian church members had each cast his vote on God's side, and therefore they were a part of the elect. How have you voted in your life?

As we go on to verses 5-10 in this chapter, we discover that in them Paul discussed the evidence which led him to believe that the Thessalonian church members were Christians.

18

Evidences of Conversion

First, according to 1 Thessalonians 1:5 he knew they were really born-again believers because they had heard the true gospel as it had been presented in the power of the Holy Spirit. "Consequently, faith comes from hearing the message, and the message is heard through the word of Christ" (Rom. 10:17).

Second, according to 1 Thessalonians 1:6 Paul knew that the Thessalonian church members were Christians because, after hearing the gospel, they received it and became imitators of him—that is, they began to live for Christ as Paul was doing. This resulted in their receiving the joy of the Holy Spirit even though they faced persecution because of their stand for Jesus Christ.

According to verse 7 Paul knew that the Thessalonian church members were truly born again because of their transformed lives. They personified Christian virtues and became examples for others to follow. They validated their faith by their actions.

Unfortunately, there are times in our day when it is impossible to tell the difference, on the basis of conduct and character, between those who claim to be Christians and those who don't. What we need to realize in this connection is that the most eloquent testimony for the Saviour is not packaged in words but in deeds. I heard a man say of another, "I know he is a Christian; his life shows it." Is that what your friends say about you?

In verse 8 Paul indicated that he knew the Thessalonian church members were Christians, because as soon as they received Christ they immediately began to tell others about Him. This desire and determination to see others saved always accompanies true conversion.

In verses 9 and 10 Paul pointed out that he knew the

Thessalonian church members were true believers because they had turned from idols to serve Christ while they waited for His return. Involvement in service while expecting Christ's return is another immutable sign of true conversion.

Several years ago Jim Cummings told me a story that beautifully illustrates all five of these evidences of conversion. The story centers around Kim S. Ton, the manager of a paper factory in Kaohsiung, Taiwan. One day while this man was riding the train from Taipei to Kaohsiung, he found a Christian magazine which someone had left on the seat beside him. He read it and was moved by the message of salvation which he found in it. When he arrived home, he sent for a year's subscription to this publication.

During that year he read the magazine with avid interest, but at the end of that time he did not renew his subscription. A year or two passed by, and he began to have family problems because he was playing the old game of "wine, women, and song."

While all this was going on, his eldest son became ill. His wife's parents called this lad a monkey boy because he was so weak and sickly; mentally he was bright, but physically he was a wreck. Because of this the in-laws suggested that he be given to the Buddhist temple. His wife, because of superstition, agreed. But the father adamantly refused; this child was the heir to all that he had.

He began to search for the answer. As he did, he discovered that Buddhism didn't have it; and so he turned from his idol. He then remembered the magazine, and the gospel it preached. He recalled that it said that one could learn more about this message at a Christian church, and that he could receive help there in the solution of his problems.

Coming home from work one night he saw the sign of the San Min Baptist Church. He wanted to go in, but he was too embarrassed to do so. However, one evening he became so desperate that he forgot his embarrassment and went to the church, earnestly seeking help. It was a Wednesday evening and the prayer service was in progress. Jim Cummings met him, got his name and address, and invited him to come to an English class on Friday. He accepted the invitation and began to attend both that class and the Sunday services regularly.

One night after an evangelistic meeting, Jim thought the time had come for Mr. Ton to respond to the gospel in the joy of the Holy Spirit. He spoke to him about it, and Mr. Ton answered in the affirmative; he invited Jesus Christ into his life as Saviour and Lord.

In speaking about this, Jim became excited as he said, "This experience completely changed Mr. Ton's personality; he became a radiant, beaming Christian, zealous to bring others to Christ." In the following years, he won his wife and son to the Saviour as well as many of his business associates. The path was not always smooth for him; he faced dark and difficult days just as the Thessalonian Christians did, but he never wavered. As he looked for the return of the Lord and contemplated it happily, he continued to serve his Master as one of the leaders of the San Min Baptist Church.

Mr. Kim S. Ton heard the gospel, and received it in the joy of the Holy Spirit despite opposition; he became a glowing example of what a Christian should be, and a faithful witness to the saving grace of Jesus Christ; he turned completely from idols. And, while he awaited the return of the Lord, he served Him faithfully. Is there any doubt about his being truly born again?

What about you? How do you measure up to this standard? Have you truly been born again? Are you really a Christian?

2
The Gospel and You

1 Thessalonians 2:1-12

When we use the term *gospel* we are usually talking about a concept or an idea rather than a tangible entity. "Preaching the gospel" means telling the good news that Jesus came, lived, died, rose again, and lives forevermore. But in reality, the gospel is not primarily a story or an idea. The gospel is first a person—Jesus Christ— in whom the gospel story finds it origin, substance and conclusion.

The thought conveyed in 1 Thessalonians 2 is the same. The gospel is first and foremost a *person*—Jesus Christ, living in and through *persons*—you and me and everyone who claims Christ as Saviour. Paul said that, in addition to the gospel story, he gave the Thessalonians his life—the gospel personified. Similarly, the gospel today is not your testimony or verbal witness, though both are valuable. The gospel is you!

Whereas Jesus Christ and the gospel story are untarnished truth, none of us Christians are. We sometimes make mistakes and, sadly, misrepresent the truth by our un-Christlike behavior. And even when it is unjustified,

Christians become—as Paul was—the targets of criticism.

Criticism is a fact of life with which every Christian has to contend. He is never free from it. Sometimes this verbal barrage is almost more than a person can bear. For example, Helen Kooiman tells the story of a high school girl who made her decision for Christ. When she went home that night, she shared with her mother the wonderful and exciting experience which had been hers. Instead of rejoicing, her mother very critically said, "I would rather have you hooked on LSD than Jesus Christ." That was tough for that new babe in Christ to take.

The Lord Jesus Christ, Himself, the only perfect person who ever lived, continually faced verbal barrages which eventuated ultimately in His crucifixion. In speaking to His disciples about this matter of criticism, He said in Luke 6:26, "Woe to you when all men speak well of you, for that is how their fathers treated the false prophets." One of the sure signs that a person is living a high quality Christian life is the criticism he receives. The more dedicated he is, the more severe that criticism will be. If there is none, then the person needs to check up on himself; in all probability his life really isn't counting for the Saviour.

What is true in our day has always been true. God's choicest servants have through the years been objects of ridicule and slander. The apostle Paul is a prime example of what I am saying. He was constantly under attack by those who sought to destroy his ministry.

In 1 Thessalonians 2:1-12 we find him answering eight implied criticisms leveled at him by the enemies of Christ.

Worthlessness and Irrelevance

The first implied criticism with which Paul deals is that

of worthlessness and irrelevance. Evidently there were those in Thessalonica who came to the Christians after Paul had left the city and said something like this: "The message that Paul, Timothy, and Silas preached to you while they were here is worthless; it is irrelevant as far as meeting your needs is concerned. Why don't you forget it?"

Paul, in answering this criticism, appealed to the believers' knowledge gained through experience as he writes, "You know, brothers, that our visit to you was not a failure" (v. 1). Our coming to you with the message of redemption was not in vain; it was not worthless and irrelevant. It met your deepest need, and today it enables you to remain steadfast in the midst of persecution. It gives you a sense of security both here and hereafter.

This accusation of worthlessness and irrelevance has always been one of Satan's main methods of attacking Christianity. Perhaps you have been influenced by this criticism, and you are on the verge of giving up your faith in Christ. You stand at the crossroads not knowing which way to turn. Before you succumb to this criticism, read this true story and apply its implications to your own life.

For a number of years my father was a successful chemist in a copper smelter in Arizona. He was also a faithful layman working hard in his church. One day he was called to be the pastor of a church in Kansas City, Missouri. After thinking and praying about it, he accepted the call, leaving behind his lucrative position.

His father was enraged by this. He criticized him unmercifully, stating that he was throwing his life away in preaching an irrelevant message.

Several years later Dad was called to Tucson, Arizona, because his father was dying of cancer. When he arrived, the doctor took a sample of his blood and found it to be the same type as his father's. He asked him if he were willing to give blood to his father, and quickly he answered yes.

In those days a transfusion was accomplished with the donor lying by the side of the recipient. As Dad lay by his father giving him blood, he said, "Dad, I love you and this is the reason I am giving you my blood. The doctor says that this will prolong your life. This is a picture of what Christ has done for us. Because of His love for man, He sacrificed His blood on Calvary as an atonement for our sins. In so doing He provided eternal life for all who believe. Don't you think the message of Christianity is relevant?"

Tears began to stream down my grandfather's face as he said, "What a fool I've been. Please forgive me. Go out and preach, with all the power you can muster, the fact that when a man is dying, as I am, the only thing that is important is his being in a right relationship with Almighty God through Jesus Christ. Yes, the message of Christianity is relevant; through it my needs are being met right now."

Character Assassination

The second implied criticism with which Paul dealt was an attempt at character assassination. There were those in Thessalonica who sought to undermine the faith of the Christians by attacking Paul's character. They probably said something like this: "They didn't tell you this, but you should know that Paul and Silas are jailbirds. So desperate were their crimes in Philippi that they were locked in the inner cell of the prison with their legs in irons. Immediately after they were released they fled here to Thessalonica and represented themselves to you as being servants of the Almighty. How can you possibly have any confidence in what they have told you? They are nothing but con artists."

In verse 2 Paul answered this: "We had previously suffered and been insulted in Philippi, as you know, but with the help of our God we dared to tell you his gospel in spite of strong opposition."

The key to understanding the significance of this verse is found in the clause, "as you know." In using it Paul was saying, "When we came to Thessalonica we told you all about our being jailed in Philippi. We found a poor girl who, because of her malady, was being used for financial gain by a group of influential Philippians. We healed her. This resulted in false charges and imprisonment for us.

"When we had a chance to escape we refused to do so, and we prevented the others from escaping. This gave us a chance to witness to the jailer and his family, and they all became Christians. In due course we were exonerated and released. The mayor of the city actually sent an entourage to escort us out of jail."

Character assassination of God's servants has been used through the years and continues to be used today as one of the most effective tools of the devil to destroy Christian work.

Every Christian worker, whether he is a layman or a clergyman, is constantly confronted with this sinister, satanic *modus operandi*. Therefore, it is important that every true believer be scrupulously careful about the manner in which he conducts himself. "Avoid every kind of evil" (1 Thess. 5:22).

Insanity
The third implied criticism of Paul was that of insanity.

His critics probably suggested that Paul had to be crazy to believe and teach that the God of the universe loved human beings so much that He sent His Son to die for them, and then raised Him from the dead.

Paul answered this criticism with one short statement in 2:3: "For the appeal we make does not spring from error." It was not of delusion, not of insanity. The implication is, "It was the real thing; it was the message that met your need and gave you peace within." It is significant that Thessalonians is not the only place in the Scripture where Paul is accused of insanity, or of deluding himself into believing something that was not true. We find the same thing in Acts 26. Paul preached the Resurrection, and Festus said, "You are out of your mind, Paul! Your great learning is driving you insane" (v. 24).

Paul was not the only Christian in the New Testament who was accused of being deluded. This same accusation was leveled at Jesus Christ by His friends. We are told in Mark 3:21 that when they heard that the multitudes were flocking to Him in order to hear Him preach and to witness the miracles which He performed that they went out to lay hold on Him. For, they said, "He is out of His mind"—He is insane.

Through the years Satan has attempted to connect the idea of insanity with the Christian message in order to keep the "thinking people" away from Christ. As long as he can convince them that it is insane to think about anything supernatural or anything that endures beyond the grave, he can block their consideration of Christian truth. The greatest thing that can happen to a person like this is to be confronted with a problem so profound and complex that he can't begin to solve it through his own rational thought processes. Then in sheer desperation he may turn to the Lord and give Him a chance. When he does, as the little chorus puts it, "Jesus never fails." The person discovers that Christianity, rather than being insane, is the revealed truth of God Himself.

A fine Christian told me this story. "While I was in college I considered Christianity and gave it up as an old wives' tale. I was sure that I could make it through life on my own. I didn't need God or anyone else to assist me. For a number of years I was successful and self-sufficient. I had all the money I wanted. I was convinced that the world was my oyster. I was really riding high.

"And then one day everything came tumbling down around me. I had tuberculosis. For six months I was flat on my back in a sanatorium. I began to think about my values in life. I discovered that they were false. In desperation I began to read the Bible and there I found what I needed— the message of Jesus Christ. I invited Him into my life as my Saviour and Lord; He came in and not only forgave my sin but delivered me from my illness.

"It made an indelible impression on me. God knocked me on my back so that I could look up!"

Friend, don't wait until God knocks you on your back before you look up. Do so now. And as you do, invite Jesus Christ into your life as your Saviour and Lord. He will accept that invitation; He will come in, transform your life, and give you citizenship in God's everlasting Kingdom.

Immorality
The fourth implied criticism is the most insidious and, for want of better terminology, the dirtiest. It is suggested in the second phrase of 1 Thessalonians 2:3, "impure motives."

The words "impure motives" come from the Greek

29

akatharsia meaning sexual immorality. Paul's critics stooped so low that they actually accused him of preaching the gospel for the purpose of attracting women to himself that he might use them for his own sensual gratification. They pictured him as the original Elmer Gantry, a man who had a good thing going for him, and he was not about to let it go.

Paul categorically refuted this criticism. In verse 10 he enlarges upon this refutation in the strongest possible language: "You are witnesses, and so is God, of how holy, righteous and blameless we were among you who believed."

Tragically, as we examine the history of Christianity we discover that there have been those so-called leaders against whom this criticism can be justifiably lodged. Such immoral men do irreparable damage to the cause of Jesus Christ. They drive people away from the Master; and they make Christianity the object of ridicule and laughter among those who have the slightest tendency toward being skeptical.

Wise, therefore, is the believer who commits both to memory and to practice Paul's command, "Avoid every kind of evil" (1 Thess. 5:22). Notice he didn't imply, "Avoid evil"; he said, "Avoid every kind of evil."

Deception

The fifth implied criticism of Paul was that he was a deceiver, one of those persons who took great delight in pulling the wool over people's eyes.

This implied criticism is found in the word "trick" in verse 3. It comes from the Greek verb *doloo* and means "to adulterate, to corrupt, or to falsify."

Paul categorically denied the validity of this criticism.

He stated, "For the appeal we make does not spring from error or impure motives, nor are we trying to trick you" (2:3). The positive implication is, "I preached Jesus Christ to you because I knew that He, and only He, could meet your basic needs and solve your problems." This is the motivation of every sincere God-called minister; he preaches because he knows that Jesus Christ has the answer to man's problems.

A lovely woman came into my office one day with a horrible black eye. Between sobs she said, "My husband, Creed, was a great football star in college, and I was one of the campus beauties. We were married during our senior year with everyone predicting great success for our home. But just the opposite is true. My husband feels that in order to be successful in business he has to hit the cocktail trail. Unfortunately he is an alcoholic. He can't stop with just one or two. Once he starts he goes the limit.

"Last night he came home drunk and started beating up on the kids. When I tried to stop him, he let me have it in the eye. Right now he is in the county jail. I have been in your church for many services; I have heard you say numerous times that if Christ is given a chance, He can meet the need of any individual. Do you think He can meet my husband's need?"

My answer was affirmative as I suggested she let me work on the case. I called a converted alcoholic and asked him to take over. He was able to get Creed paroled to him; he stayed with him 24 hours a day for the next week. During the waking hours he talked to him about Jesus.

The next Sunday Creed made his public decision for Christ. He and his family were reunited. About six months later I received from Creed's wife a Christmas card that said, "We now have a happy home; it is Christ-centered.

31

Creed takes the lead in our family devotions; he is making a great success in business without cocktails. He is the sweetest, most considerate husband a wife ever had, and the children simply adore him as their father."

You see, Christ really met that family's need; and He will meet your need if you give Him a chance.

A Man Pleaser

The sixth implied criticism of Paul was that he was seeking to please men rather than God. Paul answered this in verse 4. "On the contrary, we speak as men approved by God to be entrusted with the gospel. We are not trying to please men but God, who tests our hearts." Perhaps the criticism arose because Paul preached a gospel of liberty and joy. Legalistic minds don't enjoy hearing about freedom from the bondage of the law.

Unfortunately, there are many people today who have the same idea that Paul's critics had; they feel that the more sorrowful a person can be, the greater a Christian he is.

Christianity is anything but somber. When a person really knows Christ, he has joy and happiness in his very soul; he has a smile on his face and a song of rejoicing in his heart. This is true, regardless what his circumstances may be.

The apostle Paul was anything but comfortable in the dark and damp cell which he occupied in the Mamertine prison in Rome. His freedom of movement was greatly restricted because he was chained to a soldier. If anyone ever had a right to have a long face, Paul had it here. But instead he was the epitome of happiness. While in that situation, he wrote the letter to the Philippians, in which he told the Christians to "rejoice in the Lord" (Phil. 3:1).

One of the sure marks of a born-again Christian is the joy and happiness which exudes from him; it is contagious; it draws the attention of the people to him—and to His Lord.

A Religious Racketeer

The seventh implied criticism of Paul was that he was a religious racketeer preaching for what he could get out of it financially. This is indicated by the word "flattery" found in 1 Thessalonians 2:5. It comes from the Greek word *kolakeia* which describes flattery done in order to get something. In effect they were saying, "This guy has a good racket going for him. He plays upon people's emotions, takes an offering, and pockets the money."

Paul answered this criticism in verses 5 and 9. In verse 5 we read, "You know we never used flattery, nor did we put on a mask to cover up greed—God is our witness." Here Paul simply told his readers that God was His witness that he didn't use flattery to entice people to give him anything, nor was he the least bit greedy.

In verse 9 he stated, "Surely you remember, brothers, our toil and hardship; we worked night and day in order not to be a burden to anyone while we preached the gospel of God to you." He worked in manual labor to earn his living so that he need not take one cent from them for his ministry. He was anything but a racketeer; the criticism was absolutely unjustified.

Tragically, it is true that throughout the history of the church there have been and are religious racketeers who have made plenty of money out of fleecing the people to whom they ostensibly minister. This began before the end of the first century with various individuals traveling from city to city, claiming to be Christians and expecting the local believers to take care of their board and room.

Modern-day religious racketeers use up-to-date communications media to milk people.

Avoid being taken in. A good rule to follow is this: Never support any program not backed by an institution that has an impeccable reputation. People who follow this rule of thumb make good investments in the Lord's work, and they never get fleeced.

Personal Prestige

The eighth implied criticism of Paul was that he was egocentric, that he was in the Christian ministry for the personal prestige it gave him.

Paul answered this criticism in verses 6-8. "As for praise, we have never asked for it from you or anyone else, although as apostles of Christ we certainly had a right to some honor from you. But we were as gentle among you as a mother feeding and caring for her own children. We loved you dearly—so dearly that we gave you not only God's message, but our own lives too" *(TLB)*. Every God-called sincere, earnest preacher I have ever known has had this same attitude toward the congregation he serves. It is not his desire to be Mr. Big; instead his one supreme passion is to serve his people.

Personal prestige is nothing! Service in the name of the Saviour is everything. The person who realizes this can say with the apostle Paul, "For to me, to live is Christ and to die is gain" (Phil. 1:21).

3
It's Not an Easy Road

1 Thessalonians 2:13-20

A careful examination of 1 Thessalonians 2:13-16 reveals that Paul was dealing with three salient points that are related to basic Christianity. Each of these points centers around a pivotal word: the first is transformation, the second opposition, and the third retribution.

Transformation

Paul wrote in verse 13: "And we will never stop thanking God for this: that when we preached to you, you didn't think of the words we spoke as being just our own, but you accepted what we said as the very Word of God—which, of course, it was—and it changed your lives when you believed it" (TLB).

The Thessalonian Christians not only professed to accept Jesus Christ as Saviour and Lord, they gave evidence of it by the change that came about in their lives; their born-again experience resulted in Christlike living. They began to think, talk, and act like Christians.

This should be the norm for every believer. In Philippians 2:12,13, Paul spoke directly of this as he wrote,

"Therefore, my dear friends, as you have always obeyed—not only in my presence, but now much more in my absence—continue to work out your salvation with fear and trembling, for it is God who works in you to will and to act according to his good purpose."

Notice that Paul did not say that Christians are to work *for* their salvation; that is an impossibility. We are to work *out* our salvation; that is, we are to work out what God has worked in. When you and I accepted Christ as Saviour, the Holy Spirit came into our lives and made us new creations in Jesus. We are to manifest this for all of our friends and neighbors to see by the quality of lives that we live. This the Thessalonians did and for this Paul commended them.

Bob Bowman, one of the three founders of the Far Eastern Broadcasting Company (FEBC), told me an interesting story. A film crew studying the Shan tribal rebellion in Burma discovered that the tribespeople were involved in the opium traffic and were taking in a million dollars a year.

But they also discovered something else. The FEBC had furnished thousands of radio receivers to the Shan people, on which they received Christian broadcasts. When one of these families was converted as the result of listening to the message, the first thing they did was to quit the opium business. They changed their occupation entirely. Even though it cost them many dollars to do so, and even though getting another job was difficult, they would no longer engage in the drug racket.

When asked about it, the believers said, "Now that we are Christians we are interested in building people up, in helping people, in lifting them. All the opium trade does is to destroy them. Therefore, as believers we can have nothing whatsoever to do with it."

Those new Christians were fine examples of transformed lives.

Opposition

The material that centers around the word "opposition" is found in 1 Thessalonians 2:14-16: "And then, dear brothers, you suffered what the churches in Judea did, persecution from your own countrymen, just as they suffered from their own people the Jews. After they had killed their own prophets, they even executed the Lord Jesus; and now they have brutally persecuted us and driven us out. They are against both God and man, trying to keep us from preaching to the Gentiles for fear some might be saved; and so their sins continue to grow" *(TLB)*.

This opposition has not stopped; it is still very much with us in our day. Satan is hard at work in modern times opposing the Saviour.

In an enlightened country like ours this opposition does not express itself in overt persecution. It is not brutal; nobody is physically harmed because he is a Christian. It is far more sophisticated than that. The word that characterizes it is "indifference."

Numerous are the evidences of Western man's indifference to his only sufficient Saviour, the Lord Jesus Christ. For example, the increasing number of nude bars and pornographic films in every community in America documents this truth.

The proprietors of these businesses are completely oblivious to Jesus Christ. They live as if He never existed; their entire operation is geared to turning people away from God and His moral standards.

Another evidence of Western man's indifference to the

Lord Jesus in particular, and spiritual matters in general, is to be seen in the system of values which he has established. When you compare the amount of time and energy and money spent on sports and entertainment as opposed to the amounts spent in God-honoring activities, you see the point.

Satan has always opposed the cause of Christ, and he will continue to do so until the Lord returns.

Retribution

Notice the last part of verse 16: "But the anger of God has caught up with them at last" *(TLB)*. This is God's retribution.

As we carefully examine these words there are two truths that immediately come into focus: First, God is not only a God of love, He is also a God of wrath. Second, God, as the universal Sovereign of mankind, judges nations as well as individuals.

These truths are anything but appealing to modern man. He is much more attracted to the prevalent preaching of our day that so overemphasizes God's love that it reduces the Almighty to a senile old man who is willing to tolerate anything.

It is true that God is love; as such He has provided for man, through the death and resurrection of our Lord Jesus Christ, eternal redemption. In compassion, with arms outstretched, He invites each one of us to receive in faith this provision of His love.

But not only is God a God of love; He is also a God of wrath and judgment, and those who reject His offer of redemption will know His wrath. (See Rom. 1:18.)

God, as the Sovereign of the universe, judges nations as well as individuals. James Denney, in his book *The Epis-*

tles to the Thessalonians, suggests that Paul may have been referring to an event or act of God "in which His wrath had been unmistakably made manifest . . . . The Jews . . . had disregarded every presage of the coming storm; and at length the clouds that could not be charmed away had accumulated over their heads, and the fire of God was ready to leap out."[1]

And I would add the fire of judgment did leap out, and continues to leap out today, against Israel for her rejection of the Messiah. The Scriptures point out that there will be no end to this judgment until the tribulation period, when the Jews en masse will turn to Jesus Christ and accept Him as their Messiah.

But this message is not only for Israel, it is also for our country. God is not only the Sovereign of the Jews who live in Israel, He is also the Sovereign of the Americans who live in the United States. We, too, are subject to His judgment.

The late Francis A. Schaeffer, in his book *Death in the City,* outlined his thesis that God is judging America in this present age.

Schaeffer said, "There is only one perspective we can have of the post-Christian world of our generation: an understanding that our culture and our country is under the wrath of God."[2]

As I look at the increasing crime rate, the active divorce courts of the land, and our loss of image abroad, I see that we are like an automobile careening down a steep hill without any brakes. Unless a way is soon found to provide the needed brakes, the ultimate fatal crash is inevitable.

But there is a way out; God Himself has provided an escape hatch. He tells us about it in 2 Chronicles 7:14, "If my people, who are called by my name, will humble themselves and pray and seek my face and turn from their wicked ways, then will I hear from heaven and will forgive their sin and will heal their land." The healing of the land is dependent upon God's people, the Christians, humbling themselves before the Almighty, seeking forgiveness of sin in prayer, and becoming involved in serving the Saviour while giving up their wicked, anti-God habits. In other words, the healing of the land we love is dependent entirely upon Christians being completely turned on to the Saviour. Compromising Christians can only bring God's wrath down upon us.

Peter, in recognizing the truth of this, gave some good advice in 1 Peter 5:6,7: "Humble yourselves, therefore, under God's mighty hand, that he may lift you up in due time. Cast all your anxiety on him because he cares for you."

Sharing the Faith

When Paul was in Thessalonica on his second missionary journey, not only did he organize a church but he fell in love with the members of that church. They were his true brothers and sisters in Christ Jesus. He often thought about them and longed to see them. In 1 Thessalonians 2:17,18 he spoke about this: "But, brothers, when we were torn away from you for a short time (in person, not in thought), out of our intense longing we made every effort to see you. For we wanted to come to you—certainly I, Paul, did, again and again—but Satan stopped us."

Then in verses 19 and 20 he gives the reason for wanting to see them, and what a tremendous reason it was: "For what is our hope, our joy, or the crown in which we

40

will glory in the presence of our Lord Jesus when he comes? Is it not you? Indeed, you are our glory and joy." Paul was saying that every Christian will give an account of his stewardship to the Lord Jesus Christ at the time of His coming. He was echoing the truth of 2 Corinthians 5:10, "For we must all appear before the judgment seat of Christ, that each one may receive what is due him for the things done while in the body, whether good or bad."

In these verses, in effect, he was saying, "When I appear before the judgment seat of Christ, I shall not be there empty-handed. When I am asked to give an account of my stewardship, I shall be able to say, 'Lord, when I was in Thessalonica, I was faithful in witnessing to your saving grace. The Thessalonian Christians who stand here with me are evidence of this. In the power of the Spirit, I proclaimed your word in their city. They received it and acted upon it. These, therefore, are my hope, my joy, and my crown of rejoicing as I now stand before you.'" The number one responsibility of the Christian, as well as his highest privilege, is sharing his faith with others.

Are you daily sharing your faith with others? When you stand at the judgment seat of Christ, will you, like Paul, be able to present trophies of grace to the Master?

As you contemplate your answers to these questions, let me call to your attention two basic spiritual truths.

Be a Witness

First, if you are really a Christian, the most normal thing in the world for you to do is to witness to others about the Saviour. You will do this not because it is demanded of you, but because the love of God within you will motivate you to do so.

During the post-resurrection ministry of our Saviour,

He was being questioned one day by His disciples concerning the time schedule for the setting up of His earthly Kingdom. To those questions Jesus responded in Acts 1:7,8, "It is not for you to know the times or dates the Father has set by his own authority. But you will receive power when the Holy Spirit comes on you; and you will be my witnesses in Jerusalem, and in all Judea and Samaria, and to the ends of the earth."

Jesus did not say, "You *must* be my witnesses." There is a vast difference; one is a command, the other is a statement of fact. In these verses Jesus points out that when a person has been truly born again by the power of God's Spirit, the perfectly natural and normal thing for him to do wherever he may be is to share his faith with those with whom he comes in contact.

Peter E. Gillquist, in his book *Love Is Now,* tells the story of a small group of which he was a part addressing the members of a prominent social fraternity at UCLA. After the meeting, among several men who expressed their interest in knowing Jesus Christ, was one young man who wanted to meet with someone just as soon as possible.

Over coffee the following morning, the young man said that he would give his eyeteeth to have what the Christians had. One thing was holding him back: he was convinced that he would *have* to witness if he became a Christian. The other man assured him that God would accept him just as he was—that he could accept Christ right then, and never do a thing for the Lord, and God would still accept him.

He was so excited about the idea that he didn't have to *do* anything to win God's acceptance that he received Christ then and there.

After further conversation about the Lord, he walked back to his fraternity house. He approached the first friend he saw and said, "I've got to tell you the most amazing thing I have ever heard. Today I realized that I could invite Jesus Christ to come into my life, and that I wouldn't have to witness or do anything, and He'd still come in. This is the greatest thing I have ever heard. Isn't that fantastic?"

By evening that young man had spread the word around the entire fraternity. Because he didn't have to.[3]

People Are Hungry

Second, people everywhere, even though they don't realize it, are hungry for the gospel. They have a God-implanted thirst for truth. This is what Jesus meant when He said, "The harvest is plentiful but the workers are few. Ask the Lord of the harvest, therefore, to send out workers into his harvest field" (Matt. 9:37,38).

Today the statisticians tell us that Christianity is numerically decreasing. The reason for this is not that those outside of Christ are uninterested, for the harvest is plentiful. The reason is that the workers are few. Those who *claim* that they love the Lord are so involved in other things that they don't take time to share their faith with their friends and acquaintances.

A man in his mid-50s was dying of cancer. Listen to the confession he made to his pastor: "Pastor, 10 years ago the church asked me to teach a class of nine-year-old boys in Sunday School. I told them I was too busy—and I was, with all the heavy demands on my time and energy. I was in the prime of my life and rapidly rising in business affairs. Now, 10 years later, here I am, dying with the greatest regret of my life being that I did not accept that responsibility. I know that when I die I shall be with the Lord, but if

43

10 years ago I had taken time to teach that class of 10 boys, by now 100 boys would have passed through my class. I would have invested my life in the lives of 100 boys, and many of them would be growing in service and usefulness as Christian young men. I would have made an investment in time and eternity through them. I can't take any of my money or my stocks or my bonds with me. What a fool I have been!"

The Bible says, "He that winneth souls is wise" (Prov. 11:30, *KJV*). How wise are you?

Footnotes

1. James Denney, *The Epistles to the Thessalonians* (New York: A.C. Armstrong and Son, 1903), pp. 91-92.
2. Francis A. Schaeffer, *Death in the City* (Downers Grove: Inter-Varsity Press, 1969), p. 15.
3. Peter E. Gillquist, *Love Is Now* (Grand Rapids: Zondervan Publishing House, 1970), pp. 94,95.

4
Communicate That You Care

1 Thessalonians 3:1-13

When you really love someone you are concerned about his well-being; you desire the very best for him. When you are separated from him, you can't stand it until you learn all there is to know about his circumstances and how he is faring.

During the Vietnam war the wives of the POW's were beside themselves with anxiety about their husbands. They used every available avenue in an effort to gain information about them. Some sought help through the Red Cross and some through leaders in our government; some flew to Paris and sought audiences with the representatives of both North Vietnam and the Viet Cong. They loved their husbands and were concerned about their welfare.

This is what the third chapter of 1 Thessalonians is all about. Paul loved the Thessalonian Christians. After all, he had been instrumental in leading most of them to Christ. He and Silas and Timothy had organized them into a church. They were Paul's spiritual children. Naturally he was concerned about their well-being.

While he was away from them he began to think about them. He decided that he just had to know their true condition, so he deputized Timothy to visit Thessalonica and learn firsthand what their situation was. He also wanted him to encourage the Thessalonian Christians to remain faithful in serving the Master.

When Timothy returned with the word that they were remaining firm, that they were faithful, and that they wanted a reunion with him, naturally Paul was filled with happiness. He realized that his labor among them had not been in vain, that it had paid dividends the value of which only eternity would reveal.

Satanic Opposition

In this chapter, the Holy Spirit through Paul pulls back the curtain on two important word pictures. First, in verses 1-5 Paul graphically portrayed for us the picture of what every Christian can expect in his life.

Here the great apostle picked up the theme which is stated in 2:14-16 and enlarged on it. Simply stated, that theme is this: "The moment a person becomes a Christian, Satan begins to confront him with opposition."

A famous Nazarene evangelist, Bud Robinson, was affectionately called Uncle Bud by his friends. One day a man came to him and said, "I don't believe in a personal devil." When Uncle Bud asked why not, he responded, "Because I have never met him." Quick as a flash the evangelist retorted, "You can never meet anyone when you are traveling in the same direction he is. That's your problem. You're going the same way Satan is. But let me tell you something, old buddy. If you will do an about-face and begin to travel the Jesus road, you will meet him. As a matter of fact, you will come face to face with Satan, and

46

he will do all within his power to destroy you."

This is the point that Paul made in 1 Thessalonians 3:1-5. There are three facts concerning satanic opposition of which we should be aware.

First, Satan attacks the Christian at his most vulnerable spot. He zeroes in on his weakness. I know this on the basis of experience. My most vulnerable spot is impetuosity. I want everything done yesterday. Satan knows this and consequently he goes out of his way to plague me with what I consider to be unnecessary delays in getting the Lord's work done.

For example, just before we were ready to break ground on the senior citizens' housing unit which our church built, the court came out with a ruling that no new construction could be undertaken without an environmental impact study. This delayed the ground breaking for more than three months because no one knew what an environmental impact study was. We asked the governor's office and no one there knew what it was. The various building departments—state, county, and city—didn't know either. We struck out at the mayor's office too. I was irritated and agitated so much by this that I found myself in a constant state of fuming every day. Finally, my wife brought me up short with the question, "Why don't you practice what you preach and turn that problem over to the Lord?" Only when I did this was I able to defeat Satan; up until that time he had gained the victory.

If a Christian is having difficulty financially, Satan will hit him right at that point. He will say, "Since you are having it rough in meeting your bills with your limited income, forget about giving anything to the Lord. Let the more affluent members of the church carry the financial load. After all, you have to take care of yourself. Don't believe

47

all that stuff that the Lord will bless you if you support His work."

Unless the believer is exceedingly strong spiritually, he will easily succumb to this opposition. In so doing he will destroy his personal testimony for Christ and his usefulness for the Lord.

A good verse to remember and put into practice when Satan attacks is James 4:7: "So give yourselves humbly to God. Resist the devil and he will flee from you" *(TLB)*. Simon Peter added his "amen" to this as he declared in 1 Peter 5:8,9, "Be careful—watch out for attacks from Satan, your great enemy. He prowls around like a hungry, roaring lion, looking for some victim to tear apart. Stand firm when he attacks. Trust the Lord; and remember that other Christians all around the world are going through these sufferings too" *(TLB)*.

Second, unless the Christian is unusually alert, before he knows it, he will succumb to the attacks of the devil. This is true even of mature Christians. Simon Peter's denial of the Lord is a case in point (see Matt. 26:31-36,69-75).

No matter how mature in the faith one may be, we all have feet of clay. Paul, recognizing the truth of this, gave us some good advice in 1 Corinthians 10:12: "So be careful. If you are thinking, 'Oh, I would never behave like that'—let this be a warning to you. For you too may fall into sin" *(TLB)*.

Third, when the Christian succumbs to a satanic attack, God immediately begins to deal with him in judgment. Scripture says, "And have you quite forgotten the encouraging words God spoke to you, his child? He said, 'My son, don't be angry when the Lord punishes you. Don't be discouraged when he has to show you where you are wrong. For when he punishes you, it proves that he loves you. When he whips you it proves that you are really his child'" (Heb. 12:5,6, *TLB*). God punishes when the Christian yields to Satan. Don't overlook this; it is a basic fact of spiritual life.

A Pastor's Desire

There is a second picture in this third chapter. It is the picture of a God-called pastor's desires for the people to whom he ministers. This is seen in Paul's relationship to the Christian people in Thessalonica.

First, his desire was that they would remain faithful to Christ in the face of satanic opposition. When Timothy brought him word that such was the case, he rejoiced. Notice the way in which he expressed this in 1 Thessalonians 3:6-9: "But Timothy has just now come to us from you and has brought good news about your faith and love. He has told us that you always have pleasant memories of us and that you long to see us, just as we also long to see you. Therefore, brothers, in all our distress and persecution we were encouraged about you because of your faith. For now we really live, since you are standing firm in the Lord. How can we thank God enough for you in return for all the joy we have in the presence of our God because of you?"

A pastor's prayer is that each believer, in the face of relentless satanic opposition, will continue to remain faithful to the Saviour until He comes and takes the Church out of this world to be His holy bride.

Second, Paul wanted to have fellowship with the Thessalonian Christians around the Word of God. Paul expressed this in a unique manner: "Night and day we pray most earnestly that we may see you again and supply what is lacking in your faith. Now may our God and Father himself and our Lord Jesus clear the way for us to come to you" (vv. 10, 11).

Paul recognized that these people were studying the only Bible they had, the Old Testament. They were trying to relate its message to the person, life and ministry of Jesus Christ. He was aware that in all probability a few cracks had developed in their theology. He wanted to share with them his own insights in relating the gospel to the Old Testament.

Paul's third desire for the Thessalonians was that they might have a love relationship with one another that had a growing edge. This he expresses in verse 12, "May the Lord make your love increase and overflow for each other and for everyone else, just as ours does for you."

A little boy was once asked what a saint was. Thinking about the stained glass windows in the cathedral, he replied, "A saint is someone whom the light shines through."

Every Christian is a saint (see Rom. 1:7). As such he is to let the light of God's love shine through him as he reaches out to his fellowman, seeking to meet his needs in the name of Jesus. Such a love relationship does not go unrewarded. Paul made this clear in the last verse of the chapter: "May he strengthen your hearts so that you will be blameless and holy in the presence of our God and Father when our Lord Jesus comes with all his holy ones."

When the Lord returns, will He find that you are strong and holy, not engaging in willful sin because of your love for Him and your fellowman?

5
In Pursuit of Purity

1 Thessalonians 4:1-8

In 1 Thessalonians 4:1-8 Paul dealt with a delicate and important subject that evangelical churches too long have avoided from their pulpits; it is the subject of sexual holiness and purity. Even a casual reading of the passage reveals that Paul dealt with it in a straightforward, forthright manner. He wasn't worried about embarrassing anyone. His motivation was to instruct Christians as to God's will for them in matters of sex.

In this passage Paul issued three directives to Christians: every Christian is to be pure and holy in sexual matters; every Christian is to regard his home as a sacred and holy institution; and every Christian's mind is to be holy and clean.

Be Pure and Holy

Paul told Christians to be pure and holy in matters of sexuality (see vv. 1-5). Notice carefully that Paul was not teaching that the Christian is to be a celibate, that he is to avoid sex. He knew, as any reasonable, sensible person knows, that this relationship is one of the most beautiful,

51

one of the most mystical, one of the most satisfying relationships that God has given the human race. Paul was aware that the sex relationship was not by accident but by God's design, for the Scripture declares that He who made humanity in the beginning made us male and female.

Here Paul did not cry out against sex but against the misuse of it; it is a relationship that is reserved for husband and wife, a relationship in which they are to give themselves to one another in complete self-abandonment. Sex within the marital relationship is according to God's will; outside of that relationship it is forbidden.

We are living in a day, however, when the majority of people scoff and laugh at this biblical restriction. For them sex is no longer a private and sacred relationship for married people. Instead, it is a public and sensual relationship for anyone regardless of marital status. Even certain theological professors and so-called Christian leaders have been speaking out against God's teaching in matters of sex, advocating both free love and sexual perversion.

But, as William Barclay says, "The new morality is only the old immorality brought up to date. There is still a clamant necessity, in Britain as there was in Thessalonica, to place before men and women the uncompromising demands of Christian morality, 'for God did not call us to impurity but to consecration.'"[1]

As a servant of the living God, I place before you the fact that the Almighty demands that Christian men and women keep themselves holy and pure in sexual matters. This is an absolute standard from which God will not allow any variance; the believer who refuses to adhere to it is outside God's perfect will and can be assured that the wrath of the Almighty will in some way be meted out to him.

The Home Is Sacred

Paul directed that every Christian is to regard his home as a sacred and holy institution: "And this also is God's will: that you never cheat in this matter by taking another man's wife, because the Lord will punish you terribly for this, as we have solemnly told you before" (1 Thess. 4:6, *TLB*).

Husbands are not to cheat on their wives and wives are not to cheat on their husbands. No key club arrangement is satisfactory in God's sight; swingers are an abomination to Him. Husband and wife are to be true to each other.

Paul had a very practical reason for writing this to the Thessalonian Christians. They lived in a community that was greatly influenced by both Greek and Roman thought.

The Greeks had a very low view of marriage. Years before Paul, Demosthenes spelled it out as he said, "We keep prostitutes for pleasure; we keep mistresses for the day by day needs of the body; we keep wives for the begetting of children and for the faithful guardianship of our homes."[2] The Greeks had the philosophy that if a man supported his wife and family financially, it was perfectly all right for him to have extramarital affairs.

The attitude of the Romans was no better. Seneca put it this way, "Women were married to be divorced, and divorced to be married."

Writing in the light of this environmental influence, Paul emphasized to the Thessalonian believers that they were to repudiate it; they were to maintain homes which they looked upon as holy and sacred, homes in which marriage vows were kept, homes where genuine love prevailed.

My Greek and Roman history professor at Baylor University came to me one day just before I graduated and said, "Harold, since you are going to be a preacher, I want you to do me a favor. I am a student of Greek and Roman history. In my research I have discovered that the underlying cause for their decline and ultimate destruction was the breakup of their homes. As long as their homes were strong and impregnable, they were strong; but when their homes disintegrated, they disintegrated. And so it will be with America. As a preacher I want you to warn the people wherever you go of this basic truth, and then plead with them to regard their homes as sacred and holy."

That request was made many years ago. Since that time the domestic situation in our country has retrogressed. Today statisticians tell us that the divorce rate in our country is almost one out of two. Is it any wonder that the United States is feeling the heavy hand of divine judgment? Those of us who are married have a great responsibility before God to keep our homes strong, to regard them as sacred, holy institutions. The Bible says, "Therefore what God has joined together, let man not separate" (Matt. 19:6).

Keep Your Mind Clean

Paul directed that every Christian's mind is to be holy and clean. Notice the way he puts it in 1 Thessalonians 4:7: "For God did not call us to be impure, but to live a holy life."

Because of sin in man's life his natural inclination is to let his mind dwell on things that can tear him down morally and spiritually.

Unfortunately, in our day, much of the literature that is being produced is designed to invite the individual to fill his mind with immoral thoughts. If you don't believe this, the

54

next time you go out to dinner, look at the literature in the newspaper racks on the sidewalk just outside the front door of that eating establishment. You will discover, in 9 out of 10 of these places, filthy publications full of pornographic literature and stories.

The college director of our church took his family to a restaurant which had this type of newsrack outside. After they finished their meal he complained about the filthy literature on the sidewalk outside the door. But the restaurateur said, "Many family men have shared with me this same complaint. I have reported it to the police, but they are helpless to do anything about it." The courts of our land have refused to say that that type of literary garbage is pornographic.

In spite of all of the dirty printed material that is available, God expects and demands that we Christians keep our minds holy and clean. He tells us how we can do this in Philippians 4:8: "Finally, brothers, whatever is true, whatever is noble, whatever is right, whatever is pure, whatever is lovely, whatever is admirable—if anything is excellent or praiseworthy—think about such things." When we fill our minds with thoughts that are true, noble, right, pure, lovely and admirable, there will be no room for that which is evil and filthy.

Paul closed this section in 1 Thessalonians with a thought-provoking statement in verse 8: "If anyone refuses to live by these rules he is not disobeying the rules of men but of God who gives His Holy Spirit to you" *(TLB)*.

In and of yourself you cannot live by these rules; you must have divine help which comes only through a vital personal relationship with Jesus Christ as your personal Saviour and Lord.

Often someone will say to me, "I am going to accept Jesus Christ as my Saviour just as soon as I am sure I can live as a Christian should." To make such a statement is to put the cart before the horse. When you accept Christ by faith, the Holy Spirit takes up residence in your life. It is by His help, His assistance, His guidance, and His empowering that you are able to live by His rules.

Footnotes
1. William Barclay, *The Letters to the Philippians, Colossians and Thessalonians* (Edinburgh: The Saint Andrew Press, 1959), p. 232.
2. Ibid., pg. 231.

6
I Love You
Like a Brother

1 Thessalonians 4:9-12

Do you really want to be God's man or God's woman? Do you want it to be said of you as it was of David, "He is a person after God's own heart" (see Acts 13:22)? Do you really want this?

If your answer is yes, then you will be vitally interested in the passage we are studying in this chapter, for in it Paul made four suggestions as to how you can please God. His suggestions have a contemporary ring to them. They are: (1) Love your fellowman; (2) Keep your cool; (3) Do your own thing; (4) Work with your own hands.

Love Your Fellowman

"Now about brotherly love we do not need to write to you, for you yourselves have been taught by God to love each other. And in fact, you do love all the brothers throughout Macedonia. Yet we urge you, brothers, to do so more and more" (1 Thess. 4:9,10).

The increase of love was to include not only Christian brothers, but also those outside of Christ; even those who were their enemies and who, by pressure and persecution, were seeking to destroy their Christian witness in Thessalonica.

In making these statements the apostle Paul was echoing what the Lord Jesus Himself had said was the second greatest commandment in the law: "Love your neighbor as yourself" (Matt. 22:39).

As we think about this command of our Lord which Paul echoed, we discover that it is easy to state. It rolls off the tongue like a choice morsel, but putting it into practice is another story. That's hard! I know some Christians I have trouble even liking, much less loving; and before you jump on me about this, examine your own life and you will find the same thing to be true. The poet put it succinctly as he wrote so humorously,

"To dwell above with saints I love
To me that will be glory;
To dwell below with saints I know,
Well, brother, that's another story!"

But if we are going to be God's man or God's woman, we have to love those who are hard to like, and beyond this we must have love for our enemies. There is only one way this can be done. Jesus said it: "But I tell you: Love your enemies and pray for those who persecute you" (Matt. 5:44). *Prayer* is the key that unlocks this door.

Lt. Commander Stephen P. Harris was the intelligence officer on the *USS Pueblo* when it was captured by the North Koreans. In his book, *My Anchor Held,* he tells of his experiences as a prisoner of the communists. Shortly after the men were taken into custody, Commander Harris was told to go to his room and think about the crimes he had committed against the Korean Republic. He was forced to sit in a straight chair, at a table, under a small electric light. If he veered away from that position, guards

58

would come in and beat him. He stayed in that position all day and all night. The next morning, after 24 hours without sleep, he was instructed to write out his confession of crimes.

Let's pick up the story here as the commander tells it: "Back in my room I sat before the paper and tried to think of literary dodges. I started to doze off, then jerked my head up when I heard a guard in the corridor. I wanted to sleep, but I couldn't turn out the light. The switch was on the outside. Time crawled on. I figured the other men, especially the officers, were getting beatings, too. I wondered how they were faring. I prayed for them more than I ever had before . . . . I prayed for strength not to hate the Koreans. Scripture helped me. Fortunately, the chaplain friend who showed me the way to Christ had recommended that I enroll in the Navigators' program of Scripture memorization . . . .

"Now sitting in my room alone, trying to stay alert for the slightest noise at the door, I remembered Romans 3:23: 'For all have sinned, and come short of the glory of God.' I began feeling pity for the Koreans. 'They're slaves of a Satanic ideology and a brutal system,' I told myself. 'They're doing what they're taught to do by the system.' I reflected on the crucifixion of Christ. I prayed, 'Lord, help me to love the Koreans as you love them.'"[1]

By doing so he found the answer to his problem. He experienced dividends—the truth of 1 Corinthians 13:8, "Love never fails."

Keep Your Cool

The second suggestion that Paul made to help you be God's man or woman is to keep your cool. Notice the way he expressed it: "Make it your ambition to lead a quiet life" (1 Thess. 4:11). The Greek word from which we get "to be quiet" is *asuchazein;* one of its primary meanings is to be quiet in the sense that you don't get mad and fly off the handle, saying something for which you will be sorry later. In other words, "Keep your cool."

One of the quickest ways for a Christian to lose his influence and destroy the good he is trying to accomplish is to get mad and tell somebody off. When he does this, he not only hurts himself, but he does irreparable damage to the cause of Christ.

A fellow pastor was telling me about the ministers and churches in his area. When I asked him about a pastor he had omitted, he turned red, and almost in a fit of anger said, "That man . . . . " Then he stopped, looked up, and prayed, "Oh, Lord, set a seal on my lips!" This enabled him to regain his cool to the point that he refused to say anything about this man for whom he obviously had little respect.

All Christians would do well to pray this same prayer every time we are tempted to lose our cool. It would surely improve the quality of our testimony for the Lord.

Do Your Own Thing

"Do your own thing!" is the third suggestion Paul made to the individual who wants to be a man or woman after God's heart. Focus your attention on the second part of verse 11: "Mind your own business." The literal translation of this phrase is, "to do the things which are your own," or as the young people say, "do your own thing."

Many self-professed Christians today interpret this to mean that they can do as they please; that as long as they have their eternal fire insurance policy, everything is all right. Such, however, is not the message this phrase con-

60

veys. The Bible makes abundantly clear that the Christian's "thing" is to do the will of God; it is not what pleases him personally that is important, but what pleases the Almighty. We don't have to guess what that is. Jesus Himself spells it out for us in many places in the New Testament.

In Mark 16:15, the Saviour commanded, "Go into all the world and preach the good news to all creation." The Christian's thing is to share the gospel with everyone with whom he comes in contact. It is to let people everywhere know that Jesus Christ through His death, burial, and resurrection has made forgiveness of sins available to all who will believe.

A country doctor was greatly loved by his patients. The community in which he served was impoverished by a paralyzing depression. Many people were unable to pay their bills. When the auditor went over the books of the doctor following the physician's death, he found in numerous instances written in red, "Forgiven—too poor to pay."

The widow of the doctor was not willing to accept this. She demanded payment and took the cases to court. During the hearing the judge said to her, "Is the statement, 'Forgiven—too poor to pay' in your husband's handwriting?" When she admitted that it was, the judge responded, "It cannot be changed; it must stand as it is; no collection on your part is possible."

What a picture this is of the significance of the gospel. Justice demands that payment be made for your sin and mine. As impoverished sinners we are unable to pay. The Lord Jesus Christ, realizing this, came and died on Calvary's cross that He may do for us what we cannot do for ourselves. The moment we accept Him as Saviour, in the Lamb's *Book of Life* He writes by our name in the blood

61

red of the cross, "Forgiven—too poor to pay."

This is what the gospel is all about; we Christians do our thing by sharing this truth with others.

Work with Your Own Hands

When Paul was in Thessalonica, he preached much on the second coming of Christ. There were those who became so excited by this teaching that they began to reason something like this: "Since the Lord may come at any time, why should I work to earn a living? I'll just sit and wait for his return. If I need food, I'm sure that some of my friends and neighbors will take care of that. I will give my entire time to contemplation and worship."

Because there were so many who adopted this lifestyle, a real problem developed in Thessalonica. The working Christians found it a heavy burden to support themselves and those who refused to work. Therefore Paul, in speaking directly to this situation, wrote, " . . . and doing your own work, just as we told you before. As a result, people who are not Christians will trust and respect you, and you will not need to depend on others for enough money to pay your bills" (1 Thess. 4:11,12, *TLB*).

One of the most effective ways a man has of witnessing to his faith is by working hard and conducting himself as a Christian gentleman while so doing. Paul said, and experience documents it, that this results in his having enough money to pay his bills. It also causes those who are not Christians to trust and respect him. Often this trust and respect grows into a desire on the part of the unbelieving worker to have what the believing worker has.

A man came into my office and confessed that he was on the verge of a complete personality disintegration. He told me that he had tried to drown his troubles in liquor, but it didn't work. He told me, "The man for whom I work is an example of what I would like to be. He really applies himself to business in an honest, forthright manner, and while doing so is the epitome of compassion and love. I know that he is a Christian and goes to your church. I want what he has. Can you tell me how to get it?"

This Christian, carrying out the command of Paul, "work with your own hands," opened the door for me to witness to his employee. Before that man left my office, he invited the Saviour into his life.

God's man, God's woman, is one who loves his fellow-man, keeps his cool, does his own thing, and works with his own hands. Are you in this category?

Footnote
1. Stephen P. Harris, *My Anchor Held* (Old Tappan: Fleming H. Revell Company, 1970), pp. 31-33. Excerpts from *My Anchor Held* by Lt. Comdre. Stephen R. Harris, U.S. Navy as told to James C. Hefley are Copyright © 1970 by Fleming H. Revell Company. Used by permission.

7
Hope on Your Horizon

1 Thessalonians 4:13—5:11

President Eisenhower was asked, "How do you like growing old?" He replied, "I prefer it to the alternative." But the alternative did catch up with him. And it is going to catch up with each of us unless the Lord returns first. Both the Scripture and the experience of man document the fact that "man is destined to die once, and after that to face judgment" (Heb. 9:27).

Since this is true, every intelligent person should be vitally interested in the question, "What about the future of the dead?" In 1 Thessalonians 4:13-18 the apostle Paul addressed himself to answering this question.

Paul's Desire

Paul spoke about his desire for his Christian brothers. In verse 13 he wrote, "Brothers, we do not want you to be ignorant about those who fall asleep, or to grieve like the rest of men, who have no hope."

While Paul was in Thessalonica, he preached and taught much about the second coming of Christ. After he left the city and Christians began to die, their loved ones were upset; they did not know what the future held for them. They felt that the believer who lived until the Lord returned had nothing to fear, but they were not so sure about those who died prior to His coming. They were profoundly concerned about them.

Paul wrote 1 Thessalonians 4:13-18 to get them straightened out on this matter. He told them that his great desire for his Christian brethren was that they might be knowledgeable concerning the experience of death for the believer. In effect he said, "This knowledge will greatly reduce the intensity of your sorrow when one of your loved ones in the Lord departs this life."

There is a subtlety here that we must not miss. Paul did not tell believers that we would be free from sorrow when one of our Christian loved ones dies; he simply said that our sorrow would be much less than those who have no hope. We do have a message of comfort, consolation, and confidence to which we can cling tenaciously by faith.

There is much misunderstanding about this. For example, I have had people say to me at the funeral service of a Christian loved one, "Look at me; I should be ashamed of myself for weeping this way; I guess I am not a very good Christian."

I always answer, "Don't you believe that. The ability to weep is one of the greatest blessings God has given to man. Through tears a person releases the tension pent up within him; through tears he expresses his love for the one departed; through tears he sympathizes with all others who are in sorrow. Jesus unashamedly wept at the grave of Lazarus, and the Jews commented, 'See how he loved him!'" (John 11:36).

Those Who Die Outside of Christ

Next, Paul pictured the undesirable condition of those who die outside of Christ. This he did in two ominous words found in verse 13; two words that should make cold chills run up and down our spines: "no hope."

These words are used because once death occurs the eternal destiny of the individual is sealed; there are no second chances. Jesus made this abundantly clear in the story of the rich man and Lazarus. In it Abraham said to the unredeemed, dead rich man, "And besides all this, between us and you a great chasm has been fixed, so that those who want to go from here to you cannot, nor can anyone cross over from there to us" (Luke 16:26). There are no second chances. The words "no hope" describe the eternal condition of every person outside of Christ.

The Righteous Dead

"We believe that Jesus died and rose again and so we believe that God will bring with Jesus those who have fallen asleep in him" (1 Thess. 4:14). The New Testament 14 times describes death for the Christian as "sleep." Not only is this found in the New Testament, but also in the Old. The prophet Daniel, in referring to those who would take part in the bodily resurrection, designated them as those who sleep in the dust of the earth.

Dr. Alexander MacLaren, the famous Bible expositor, points out that sleep has two connotations in the Scripture. First, it has the connotation of rest, and second, the connotation of a glorious awakening.[1] This is exactly what Paul had in mind, I believe, in using this phrase. At the point of death, as far as the physical body is concerned for the Christian, there is rest, but as far as his soul is concerned, there is a glorious awakening. "Away from the body . . . at home with the Lord" (2 Cor. 5:8).

You and I who have loved ones who are dead in Christ need to recognize that in reality they are asleep through Christ; for through the power of Christ their bodies are at rest, but they themselves are with the Lord. What a glorious and comforting thought this is. Is it any wonder that Paul said he didn't want us "to grieve like the rest of men, who have no hope."

Eternal Assurance

Paul wrote, "We believe that Jesus died and rose again" (1 Thess. 4:14). In effect, he was saying: "This great promise that I have given you, that the Christian is absent from his body and is at home with the Lord, and the one that I am about to give you of ultimate victory through the Second Coming, is completely dependent upon your willingness and faith to accept the fact that Jesus Christ died for your sins and that He was raised again from the dead for your justification." The one thing that makes a difference as far as eternity is concerned is your faith in the Lord Jesus Christ.

Dr. Herschel Fort of the First Baptist Church of El Paso, Texas, tells the story of a father who was lying on his deathbed. As his three sons gathered around, the father said to the first two, who were Christians, "Goodbye, sons, I'll see you in the morning and we will have a wonderful experience where there will be no separation again for us." Turning to the third son, who had never accepted Christ as his Lord and Saviour, the father said with finality, "Good-bye, son."

This son was greatly touched by that experience and he said to his father, "Why did you tell me good-bye with such finality when you said to my brothers, 'I'll see you again'?"

The father said, "Because, son, there is one thing that makes a difference in eternity and that is faith in Jesus Christ as Lord and as Saviour. Your brothers have accepted Christ as Saviour. But you, my son, resolutely have determined in your heart not to accept Jesus Christ as your Saviour. The thing that hurts me most in going out into eternity is the fact that I know I'll never see you again."

This son began to weep, and as he wept he said, "Oh, father, tell me how." And as the father talked to his son, he said, "If you will just exercise childlike faith in Christ, then someday our family will be complete in eternity through Christ Jesus."

The boy did accept Christ; and just before the father left this earth he could say to the third son, as he had to the first two, "Good-bye, my son, I'll see you in the morning."

The Return of the Lord

The most dynamic words found anywhere in literature are those which Paul used in verses 15-18 to describe the return of the Lord for His Church, the event known in evangelical circles as "the rapture."

Here he writes, "According to the Lord's own word, we tell you that we who are still alive, who are left till the coming of the Lord, will certainly not precede those who have fallen asleep. For the Lord himself will come down from heaven, with a loud command, with the voice of the archangel and with the trumpet call of God, and the dead in Christ will rise first. After that, we who are still alive and are left will be caught up with them in the clouds to meet the Lord in the air. And so we will be with the Lord forever. Therefore encourage each other with these words."

As we look carefully at this statement we discover that there will be three sounds accompanying our Lord's return.

First there will be a shout from the Lord Himself. This will be heard by everyone who is asleep in Christ. There is a graphic prefiguring of the power of this voice in the earthly ministry of our Saviour. As He stood outside the tomb of Lazarus, He shouted, "Lazarus, come out!" And Lazarus came forth (see John 11:43).

When He comes for the Church, every dead believer will hear that shout and will emerge victorious over the grave.

The voice of the archangel will also be heard as He comes. Hebrews 1:14 suggests that the moment a person becomes a Christian, he is assigned an angel to minister to him. As the Lord returns, the archangel will be giving orders to the ministering angels to take care of those to whom they have been assigned, making sure that every detail has been cared for in preparing them for their rapture.

The third sound will be that of the trumpet of God. In the Old Testament days trumpets were used to call the people of Israel together to a holy convocation. It is in this manner that the trumpet of God will be used in that day. Gabriel will sound the trumpet, and all of God's people will respond. What a holy convocation that will be. At that time we shall look upon the face of our Lord and adore and worship Him. This is what Paul meant when he wrote in 1 Corinthians 13:12, "Now we see but a poor reflection; then we shall see face to face." Now by faith we see our Lord dimly, but when the rapture occurs this will all be changed. We will see Him face to face.

Many years ago when Billy Graham was in Korea, he visited a Naval hospital. There he went from bed to bed, meeting the boys, talking to them and praying with them. While doing this, he came to a marine who had been wounded in the back and consequently was forced to lie facedown.

As Billy talked to him the young man said, "I have heard you preach over the radio, but I have never seen your face, which I would very much like to do. You are an inspiration to me; I have come to know the Lord through your preaching."

Quick as a flash Billy lay down on his back under this man's cot. In that position the two viewed one another face to face. And the marine said, "Thank you, Billy, for what you mean to me."

As Christians you and I have heard the voice of Jesus through the ministry of the Holy Spirit in our lives. And this has been wonderful. But when He comes for us, it will be even better. For then each of us will be privileged to look into His face.

In 1 Thessalonians 5:1-11 the apostle Paul discussed that which is known in theology as the doctrine of eschatology, or the doctrine of last things. This all centers around the phrase, "the day of the Lord," found in verse 2. Even a cursory reading of these verses reveals that we cannot begin to comprehend what the apostle is teaching in them unless we have an understanding of the biblical meaning of this phrase. "What is the day of the Lord?" is the pivotal question.

In searching the Scriptures for an answer to it, we discover that there are at least ten basic facts revealed about it.

The Day of the Lord

First, the Bible teaches us that it is not just a 24-hour period. In 2 Peter 3:8 the big fisherman wrote, "With the

71

Lord a day is like a thousand years, and a thousand years are like a day." This particular statement pertains to the day of the Lord. It is not limited by minutes or days or weeks; it is not limited by years or decades—it is not even limited by centuries. It is a period of indeterminate length.

Second, "the day of the Lord" is a period of time in which many major events are going to take place. From 2 Peter 3:10-13 and Revelation 4—21, we learn that these events are: the period of great tribulation, the second coming of Christ, the battle of Armageddon, the judgment of the nations, the judgment of God upon Israel, the millennial reign of the Saviour, the final defeat of Satan, the second resurrection, the judgment of the great white throne, the destruction of the present heavens and the earth, and the establishing of the new heaven and earth.

In commenting on this, Dr. Lewis Sperry Chafer wrote, "It may then be seen that this day includes the judgments of God upon the nations and upon Israel and that these judgments occur at Christ's return . . . . It extends indeed to the final dissolution with which the kingdom ends."[2]

Third, "the day of the Lord" is immediately preceded by "the day of Christ." Unlike "the day of the Lord," "the day of Christ" is a very brief span of time. It refers to that moment when the Lord Jesus is going to come and take His bride, the Church, out of the world. In popular theological jargon it is called "the rapture." Paul, in referring to this event, points out that it will occur "in a flash, in the twinkling of an eye" (1 Cor. 15:52).

Fourth, with the exception of the millennial period, "the day of the Lord" will be characterized by war and violence. Joel spells this out so simply that even a child can understand it: "Proclaim this among the nations: Prepare for war! Rouse the warriors! Let all the fighting men draw near and attack. Beat your plowshares into swords and your pruning hooks into spears. Let the weakling say, 'I am strong!' Come quickly, all you nations from every side, and assemble there. Bring down your warriors, O Lord! 'Let the nations be roused; let them advance into the Valley of Jehoshaphat, for there I will sit to judge all the nations on every side. Swing the sickle, for the harvest is ripe. Come, trample the grapes, for the winepress is full and the vats overflow—so great is their wickedness!' Multitudes, multitudes in the valley of decision! For the day of the Lord is near in the valley of decision. The sun and moon will be darkened, and the stars no longer shine. The Lord will roar from Zion and thunder from Jerusalem; the earth and the sky will tremble. But the Lord will be a refuge for his people, a stronghold for the people of Israel" (Joel 3:9-16).

Fifth, the Bible reveals that beginning at the midpoint of the tribulation period and continuing throughout that period of "the day of the Lord" the Jews will turn en masse to Jesus Christ as their Messiah. Some people today tell us that God is through with the Jews. They contend that because the people of Israel for the most part rejected Christ in His first coming and continue to do so today, the Almighty has no further place for them in His economy.

This is not the case. The trickle of Jews today who are turning to Jesus as Messiah will become a mighty river during "the day of the Lord." Paul raises the question, "Hath God cast away his people?" And he answers, "God forbid . . . . God hath not cast away his people which he foreknew" (Rom. 11:1,2, *KJV*). God loves the Jews today just as much as He did during the days of the Old Testament; they are just as near to His heart as they ever have

73

been; and they shall continue to be so.

The prophet Jeremiah talks about what is going to happen during "the day of the Lord" as far as Israel is concerned. He refers to their persecution during this period as the time of Jacob's distress. "How awful that day will be! None will be like it. It will be a time of trouble for Jacob, but he will be saved out of it" (Jer. 30:7). Here Jeremiah informs us that during "the day of the Lord" the people of Israel are going to suffer severe persecution. The book of Revelation describes the truth of Jacob's trouble, of Israel's persecution. They are going to be harassed, incarcerated, and martyred more during this period than ever before in history. But God tells us that they are going to be saved out of it. "'In that day,' declares the Lord Almighty, 'I will break the yoke off their necks and will tear off their bonds; no longer will foreigners enslave them. Instead, they will serve the Lord their God and David their king, whom I will raise up for them'" (Jer. 30:8,9).

Just at the time the persecution is about to become its severest, the Almighty is going to step back into history in the Person of our Lord Jesus Christ, save Israel from her enemies by defeating them at the battle of Armageddon, and begin His earthly reign seated on David's throne.

See the picture portrayed here. During the millennium Jesus Christ as King of kings and Lord of lords will be the world's benevolent dictator. The Jews who turned to Him en masse during the last part of the tribulation period, and the Jews who during this age of grace acknowledge Him as Messiah will be serving Him. They will be most prominent in His Kingdom.

Sixth, "the day of the Lord," with the exception of the millennial reign, will be a time of wrath and judgment. Zephaniah writes, "The great day of the Lord is near—

74

near and coming quickly. Listen! The cry on the day of the Lord will be bitter, the shouting of the warrior there. That day will be a day of wrath, a day of distress and anguish, a day of trouble and ruin, a day of darkness and gloom, a day of clouds and blackness, a day of trumpet and battle cry against the fortified cities and against the corner towers. I will bring distress on the people and they will walk like blind men, because they have sinned against the Lord. Their blood will be poured out like dust and their entrails like filth. Neither their silver nor their gold will be able to save them on the day of the Lord's wrath. In the fire of his jealousy the whole world will be consumed, for he will make a sudden end of all who live in the earth" (Zeph. 1:14-18).

Seventh, the Bible teaches that it is impossible to set the exact day when the rapture of the Church will take place and "the day of the Lord" will begin. "Now, brothers, about times and dates we do not need to write to you" (1 Thess. 5:1). The reason is obvious. This is privileged information. According to Acts 1:7 "the day of the Lord" is known only to the Father.

Eighth, "the day of the Lord" will come quickly and without warning. "For you know very well that the day of the Lord will come like a thief in the night" (1 Thess. 5:2). When that moment according to God's time schedule arrives for the rapture of the Church, suddenly the believers will all be gone from the earth, and "the day of the Lord" will come upon those who remain.

Ninth, the Bible informs us that "the day of the Lord" will come when people are talking much about peace. Notice verse 3: "While people are saying, 'Peace and safety,' destruction will come on them suddenly, as labor pains on a pregnant woman, and they will not escape."

Peace is the number one topic of conversation in our day. As a matter of fact, there has never been a time in the history of the world when men have talked more about this subject and been able to do less about it. I need only mention the Middle East to document the truth of this. We need to apply seriously verse 3. Men are crying peace and safety. The question is, "When will destruction come upon them?" And the answer is, "It could come at any time."

Tenth, the Bible teaches that when "the day of the Lord" comes, there will be no place for those who reject Christ to hide from God's wrath which will be poured out upon the earth. Notice the last part of verse 3, "And they will not escape." *The Living Bible* translates it, "There will be no place to hide."

Many Americans today have apparently everything—fine cars, lovely homes, elegant clothes, plenty of money, and rich food. There is nothing wrong with this, but some of these people conduct themselves as if God does not exist and as if they are never going to give an account to the Lord Jesus Christ for their actions. These people don't attack Christ; they simply live in oblivion to His claims and to what He has done for them. In Revelation 6:15-17 we are told that people like this will go to the mountains, and they will cry out, "Fall on us and hide us from . . . the wrath of the Lamb!" (v. 16). This prayer will be in vain; for there will be no place to hide.

Paul's Admonitions

In the light of what the Bible reveals about "the day of the Lord," Paul gave us three admonitions.

First, he told us to be alert to the fact that "the day of the Lord" is going to come. Christians can be assured that just as night follows day, as darkness follows light, just so when that moment on God's time schedule is reached for "the day of the Lord" to begin, it will begin.

"But you, brothers, are not in darkness so that this day should surprise you like a thief. You are all sons of the light and sons of the day. We do not belong to the night or to the darkness. So then, let us not be like others, who are asleep, but let us be alert and self-controlled. For those who sleep, sleep at night, and those who get drunk, get drunk at night" (1 Thess. 5:4-7).

The practical reason for this admonition should be apparent to all of us. The Christian who lives daily with the thought that the Lord may come at any moment is going to concentrate on keeping his life clean and his testimony above reproach so that he will not be ashamed when he meets his Saviour face to face. John echoed this same thought. "Everyone who has this hope in him purifies himself, just as he is pure" (1 John 3:3).

The first time our elder daughter, Mary, and her husband, Randy, visited us after their marriage, my wife prepared for their visit by working night and day to clean the house. She went over every nook and cranny with a fine-tooth comb. In anticipation for our loved ones' coming, there was motivation for those long hours of housecleaning.

And so it is regarding the rapture of the Church and the beginning of "the day of the Lord." Those who are looking for these events are going to keep their lives clean and their testimonies above reproach.

Second, Paul told us to make sure that our conversion to Christ is more than just an emotional experience. "But since we belong to the day, let us be self-controlled, putting on faith and love as a breastplate, and the hope of salvation as a helmet. For God did not appoint us to suffer wrath but to receive salvation through our Lord Jesus Christ. He died for us so that, whether we are awake or asleep, we may live together with him" (1 Thess. 5:8-10).

As an old Scotsman lay dying, someone spoke to him about his salvation, asking whether or not he had made his peace with the Father through the Son. His answer was a classic: "Aye, man, I thatched my house when the weather was warm."

Third, Paul told us to comfort and encourage each other with the fact that "the day of the Lord" is going to come and will have a threefold result. First, evil will be defeated; Satan and his cohorts will be smashed. Second, Christ will be acknowledged as King of kings and Lord of lords. Third, every Christian will share in the glory of His eternal Kingdom.

A man who had rejected Christ most of his life finally received Him during his final illness. His wife and daughters didn't know about it until I spoke with them a few minutes before the funeral. Tears of joy filled their eyes when they heard the news, and they said, "What a comfort this news is!"

Yes, it is comforting to know that when one of your Christian loved ones departs this life he goes to share with Christ the glory of His eternal kingdom. If you were to die right now, would the members of your family have this comforting assurance about you?

Footnote
1. Alexander MacLaren, *Expositions of Holy Scripture* (Grand Rapids: Baker Book House, 1974), pp. 186-198.
2. Lewis Sperry Chafer, *Systematic Theology* (Dallas: Dallas Seminary Press, 1948), Vol. VII, p. 110.

8
When All Else Fails, Follow Instructions

1 Thessalonians 5:12-28

One of the great characteristics of 1 Thessalonians is its practicality. It speaks to the Christian in terms of everyday life. This is especially true in 5:12-28, the very last part of the book. Here Paul gave us a list of 18 practical exhortations designed to improve the quality of our lives.

Be Patient

Paul said, "Be patient with everyone" (v. 14). The question arises, "What does the word 'patient' actually mean?" To begin with, the word "patient" means "waiting." But it means more than that, especially in the way the Bible uses the term. The verbal form "be patient" comes from the Greek word *makrothumeite,* which literally means "to be patient in bearing the offense of others," or, "to be mild and slow in avenging, to be longsuffering, to be slow to anger, to be slow to punishment, to defer punishment." Solomon got at the root of the meaning of this word when he wrote, "A man's wisdom gives him patience" (Prov. 19:11).

A preacher trying to define it in modern terms said, "Patience is the ability to idle your motor when you feel like stripping your gears."

Yes, to be patient is more than just to wait; it is to defer anger and punishment.

A famous doctor performed a tracheotomy on a patient and then turned him over to a nurse for special care. The line leading to the patient's throat became clogged. Instead of keeping her cool, the nurse panicked and the patient died.

The doctor was livid with anger, and rightfully so. He said to the nurse, "I am going to have your license revoked. I am going to see to it that you never take care of another patient."

The nurse replied, "Doctor, I am a Christian. I am convinced that God has called me to be a nurse. I know that I shouldn't have panicked; I have no excuse; you have every right to take disciplinary action. But if you will give me one more chance I will guarantee that it will never happen again. Please be patient with me."

Brusquely the doctor answered, "I'll have to sleep on it."

The next morning when he awakened, as a Christian he felt that the Holy Spirit was leading him to give that nurse another chance, and so he did. In a few years she became one of the most respected nurses in the hospital, and ultimately became superintendent of nurses. He deferred his punishment, and the nurse made good.

This is a picture not only of the way in which Christians should deal with one another, but also of the way in which God has constantly dealt with non-Christians, and continues to do so today. He is deferring judgment.

In 2 Peter 3:1-9 the big fisherman talked about this in

relationship to the second coming of Christ. He told us about a number of scoffers who were making fun of the idea that Christ would return. They were saying that ever since the beginning of time things have continued as they were; therefore, it is ridiculous for anyone to believe that Jesus will come back to earth.

Simon Peter answered them by saying that one day with the Lord is as a thousand years and a thousand years as one day. And then he declared, "The Lord is not slow in keeping his promise, as some understand slowness. He is patient with you, not wanting anyone to perish, but everyone to come to repentance" (v. 9).

This principle not only applies to the second coming of Christ, but also to the non-Christian's death. The Bible makes it clear that every individual deserves death (see Rom. 6:23). If God meted out justice to humanity right now, not one single person would draw another breath.

But God deals with each individual on the basis of patience; He is deferring punishment in order that each of us might make his decision for Christ, thereby being prepared for eternity.

This is not the whole story, however. There is a limit to God's patience. In Genesis 6:3 He says, "My Spirit will not contend with man forever." There comes a point in time when every person who turns his back constantly on Christ sins away his day of grace; he pushes the Lord's patience beyond its limit for him. When that moment is reached, that person dies, and dying without Christ means eternal hell.

Every nonbeliever needs to look at this truth. God is patient with him; He is sparing his life so that he can prepare for eternity through faith in Jesus Christ. The one who is wise will take advantage of this by making that decision which means the difference between life and death, between heaven and hell.

Avoid Evil

The second exhortation is "Abstain from all appearance of evil" (1 Thess. 5:22, *KJV*). *The Living Bible* translates this, "Keep away from every kind of evil."

Here Paul was simply pointing out what every one of us knows to be true. If we play with fire, we are going to be burned; if we play games with evil, it will lead to destruction. Wise is the person who does not make the initial move toward the sin that can destroy him. Wise is that person who not only avoids evil but even the appearance of it.

In our day we have many false teachers who are saying that this is not true; that this doctrine went out with the horse-and-buggy days; that modern sophisticates cannot and must not accept it. They contend that there are certain activities we can enjoy that will neither destroy us as persons, nor hurt our influence; instead they will give us sensual pleasure to which we are entitled.

Many self-styled teachers today are telling us there is nothing wrong in smoking pot; they contend that it does not lead to the use of harder narcotics; that it is not habit forming in any way. They argue that it gives us a euphoric feeling and that this is a pleasure to which all of us are entitled.

This is the devil's lie. It may be proven scientifically that it is not habit forming, but by the same token it can be shown experientially that it does lead to the use of harder narcotics which destroy.

George Putnam, a long-standing television journalist in Los Angeles, did a research project in which thousands of heroin addicts were interviewed. In almost every case the addict stated that he began smoking marijuana or using one of the lesser narcotics and this led him on to the use of the harder stuff.

Another study found that "25 percent of the 6,500 drug addicts interviewed . . . followed this four-step sequence toward addiction: first, marijuana; second, amphetamines (speed); third, barbiturates; and fourth, heroin. The other 75 percent skipped one or two steps, but none went directly to heroin without first using one of the other drugs."

The research for this article was done through "Friends of Psychiatric Research, Inc." of Baltimore, among addicts ranging in age between 13 and 74 in New York City, Chicago, Los Angeles, Washington, D.C., San Antonio and Tacoma. All who were interviewed were addicts who had been treated at federally financed medical centers.

These heroin users did not start out to be addicts when they smoked that first joint or took that first upper or downer. They were simply looking for that first euphoric feeling they thought they were entitled to. Had they listened, however, to Paul's exhortation to keep away from evil of every kind, they wouldn't be in the trouble they are today. They played with fire, and they were burned.

This principle applies not only to narcotics but to every evil, including alcohol. No alcoholic ever started out to be an alcoholic; he started out to be a social drinker, to be one of the boys. He learned how to curl his little finger just right and to tell off-color stories so he could be part of the "in" crowd. He found, however, when he started, he couldn't stop; and the final result was tragic. Had he never taken his first drink, the story would have been different.

And this is not all; a postscript needs to be added for parents. If you as a parent drink in your home, and thereby give your child the impression that drinking is OK, you are doing him a great disservice. One out of every seven people is a potential alcoholic; your child may be one of these. If he begins to drink because of your influence, and he is an alcoholic, it won't be long until he blows his mind and ruins his life. The fault will not be his but yours. His blood will be on your hands; God will hold you accountable for it because you are your brother's keeper.

Paul's exhortation in 1 Thessalonians 5:22 really applies here. "Avoid every kind of evil," including booze and narcotics. Nobody ever got in trouble from alcohol by leaving it alone, nor from dope by having nothing to do with it. And do you know how to do this? By complete surrender of yourself to the lordship of Christ and the daily control of the Holy Spirit.

The finale of 1 Thessalonians is found in 5:12-28. In these verses Paul shared with us 18 practical exhortations which every Christian would do well to practice daily. Such practice will result in the believer living above the line of compromise, and consequently having a testimony which the Spirit of God can and will use in turning people to Jesus Christ.

Let us look at these 18 exhortations as they are translated in *The Living Bible*. Most of them are self-explanatory and need no amplification. They zing their way into our minds and hearts; they challenge us to be the Christians God wants us to be.

"Dear brothers, honor the officers of your church who work hard among you and warn you against all that is wrong. Think highly of them and give them your wholehearted love because they are straining to help you. And remember, no quarreling among yourselves. Dear brothers, warn those who are lazy; comfort those who are frightened; take tender care of those who are weak; and be patient with everyone. See that no one pays back evil for evil, but always try to do good to each other and to everyone else. Always be joyful. Always keep on praying. No matter what happens, always be thankful, for this is God's will for you who belong to Christ Jesus" (vv. 15-18).

Don't Pay Back Evil

Let's zero in on three of Paul's exhortations. First, "See that no one pays back evil for evil, but always try to do good to each other and to everyone else" (v. 15, *TLB*).

In this verse Paul exhorted us to do what is seemingly impossible. He was saying, "When someone wrongs you, even if he doesn't ask for it, you are to forgive him. Then prove that you have done so by going out of your way to do something nice for him."

To comply with this is most difficult because it runs contrary to our Adamic natures. When someone strikes out against us, our immediate reaction is to strike back, to get even.

This is not the spirit of Christ. Simon Peter, in referring to Him, wrote, "Christ suffered for you, leaving you an example, that you should follow in his steps. 'He committed no sin, and no deceit was found in his mouth.' When they hurled their insults at him, he did not retaliate; when he suffered, he made no threats. Instead, he entrusted himself to him who judges justly" (1 Pet. 2:21-23).

When Christ was insulted, He did not answer back. As Isaiah put it, "As a sheep before her shearers is silent, so he did not open his mouth" (Isa. 53:7). His enemies hurled insult after insult at Him, and yet our Lord did not say one word in response.

And so it should be with each of us. So it is with the truly great and productive Christians. A case in point is that of Billy Graham. No minister of the gospel has ever been more maligned than Billy. He gets it from both sides: from the extreme fundamentalists and from the extreme liberals. But he never answers back.

When Christ suffered, He never threatened to get even. He could have done more than threaten; He could have gotten even, for He is God (see Matt. 27:54). But, instead, He forgave those who wronged Him, without their asking Him to do so. On the cross, when He looked down and saw those who were responsible for His execution, He cried out, "Father, forgive them, for they do not know what they are doing" (Luke 23:34). He not only forgave them, but He went on to die for them and then to conquer death to make available to them the gift of everlasting life.

In Christ's attitude toward those who insulted Him, and in His attitude toward those who caused Him to suffer, He is the example that God expects every Christian to emulate.

Each one of us needs to be like a German refugee about whom Oswald Hoffman tells. His mother and father were shot down in cold blood by Soviet guards, who later offered the explanation that these aged people were trying to flee through the snow. When he was asked about his attitude toward the Russians, he said in effect, "As a Christian, what am I to do but forgive?" Paul exhorted us to: "See that no one pays back evil for evil, but always try to do good to each other and to everyone else." This Ger-

86

man refugee has implemented this exhortation in his life. Have you?

Be Joyful

In the sixteenth verse Paul said, "Be joyful always." It is the joyful, happy Christian whose testimony is magnetic; it is he whom the Spirit of God uses to draw others to the Saviour.

A believers who has a sour personality just can't get the job done. He repels rather than attracts; he is one of the most effective instruments the devil has in his service. Other Christians don't even want to be around him, much less unbelievers.

You and I are to be happy, rejoicing Christians, magnetic in our appeal to others in behalf of the Saviour. In order for us to be this, two things are of the greatest importance. First, we must realize that God in Christ Jesus really loves us as persons. Only the consciousness of God's love in Jesus Christ can make us perfectly happy.

This is what the late Clarence Macartney had in mind when he wrote under the caption, "Where Is Happiness?"

"Not in unbelief—Voltaire was an infidel of the most pronounced type. He wrote, 'I wish I had never been born.'

"Not in pleasure—Lord Byron lived a life of pleasure, if any one did. He wrote: 'The worm, the canker, and the grief are mine alone.'

"Not in money—Jay Gould, the American millionaire, had plenty of that. When dying he said, 'I suppose I am the most miserable man on earth.'

"Not in position and fame—Lord Beaconsfield enjoyed more than his share of both. He wrote: 'Youth is a mistake, manhood a struggle; old age a regret . . . . '

"Not in military glory—Alexander the Great conquered the known world in his day. Having done so, he wept in his tent, because, he said, 'There are no more worlds to conquer.'

"Where, then, is happiness found? The answer is simple. 'In Christ alone.' He said, 'I will see you again, and your heart will rejoice, and your joy no man taketh from you.'" (See John 16:22, *KJV*.)

Second, we must involve ourselves in serving our Lord Jesus. Inactivity always breeds discontent, while activity contributes to our happiness in the Saviour. My authority for saying this is Jesus, Himself, who declared in John 13:17, "Now that you know these things, you will be blessed if you do them."

Is your joy full? Are you a happy Christian?

Pray

Paul said, "Pray continually." The King James translates this exhortation, "Pray without ceasing" (1 Thess. 5:17).

The wife of an outstanding Presbyterian minister confessed that for years she was bothered by this verse. She thought it meant that she was to spend hours and hours upon her knees in supplication and intercession. This she knew was an impossibility in view of the many household duties she had to perform in taking care of her husband and four children. As she thought about this the answer came to her. She realized, "I can pray when I am washing the dishes, when I am cleaning the house, when I am driving the kids to school, and when I am preparing for the many responsibilities I have at church." When she began to put this idea into practice she discovered that she was literally living in the presence of the Lord; and the blessings that she received were tremendous.

Let me suggest that the next time a difficulty arises in your life and you don't know where to turn, quietly talk to the Lord about it. Give Him a chance to help. You won't be disappointed; you will be pleased with what will happen, for you will experience the truth that Robert Browning pointed out when he said, "More things are wrought by prayer than this world dreams of."

And when we pray we are not only to ask God for things, but we are to thank Him for what He has done for us. Notice verse 18: "Give thanks in all circumstances, for this is God's will for you in Christ Jesus." Many Christians completely overlook this facet of prayer. They have the "give me's," not the "thank you's." They are like the nine lepers rather than the one who returned to thank the Saviour for healing them. When we pray we should thank Him for the specific blessings He has given us—for our salvation in Christ, for the air that we breathe, the cars we drive, the food we eat, the clothes we wear, and the homes in which we live. We should thank Him for our loved ones, for our church, for our jobs, for our health, and for our friends. In all things, not just some things, we are to give thanks for this is the will of God for the Christian.

The theme of praise, thanksgiving, and blessing is emphasized again and again throughout the Scripture. It is very much in evidence both in the Old and New Testament.

For example David sings out: "Praise the Lord, O my soul; all my inmost being, praise his holy name" (Ps. 103:1).

The apostle Paul, incarcerated in the Mamertine prison in Rome, wrote, "Rejoice in the Lord always. I will say it again: Rejoice!" (Phil. 4:4). He knew that it is the will of God for you and me to praise the Lord in all circumstances. He not only practiced this himself, but he challenged us to do the same.

Make no mistake about it. One of the secrets of entering into the abundant life that is offered in Christ is being able to praise and thank God in all circumstances.

This is a difficult concept for many Christians to grasp because it seems on the surface so illogical. I must confess my own difficulty. I have been in the ministry for more than 45 years. During all of this time 1 Thessalonians 5:18 has been in the Bible. But for 36½ years it was just a theory to me, which I felt applied only to the first-century Christians. I didn't see how it could have any place in the life of one living in our time. I had no difficulty in praising God and thanking Him for the blessings that came into my life. But for the difficulties, the crises, the emergencies— no way!

Then I had a refreshing experience with the Holy Spirit in which He enabled me to see that this concept is as much for our day as it was for the apostle Paul's. And how thankful I am for this! It has enabled me to live on the victory side of life ever since that time. I know for sure that I am to praise the Lord in every situation.

I know it from the standpoint of the experience of others. In 2 Corinthians 8, for example, we find Paul holding up the members of the three Macedonian churches— Philippi, Thessalonica, and Berea—as exhibit "A" as to how Christians should give to the Lord. In verse 2 he writes, "Out of the most severe trial, their overflowing joy and their extreme poverty welled up in rich generosity."

A careful analysis of this verse reveals that Paul points out four characteristics of these first-century Christians. He presents these in couplets, each portraying a contrast.

In the first couplet he tells us that these Christians were persecuted. His actual wording is, "out of the most severe trial." From the moment Paul and Silas organized these churches, the persecution began. In Philippi he and Silas were put in jail; in Thessalonica and Berea they were run out of town. This was a foretaste of what the members of these churches constantly faced. If I had been one of them I would have felt sorry for myself and would have wondered if God had forgotten me. But they didn't! In the face of persecution they abounded in joy. The word used literally means "superabounded." They praised the Lord and thanked Him for the hardships with which they were confronted.

The second couplet speaks of their being impoverished on the one hand and giving liberally on the other. I am convinced that they were able to do this because they praised their Saviour in every circumstance.

In a prayer meeting a beautiful young housewife said, "My husband was arrested on a narcotics charge. When I heard about it, I praised the Lord. And the most wonderful thing has happened. God had turned what could have been a horrible nightmare into a blessing. My husband found the Lord. When I visit him now we don't count the days until he is released. Instead, we praise the Lord for His goodness and then ask the Saviour to give him the same type of ministry during the year of his sentence that Paul had while he was in jail."

As I looked at this young lady I learned from her the value of putting into practice 1 Thessalonians 5:18.

But not only do I see the value in this observing others, I have experienced it myself. I have a mild case of diabetes. One summer while on vacation I cheated a little on my diet, thinking I could get by with it.

But the day of reckoning came. When I had my blood sugar checked I found that I was 170 points too high. Ordinarily in that situation I would have felt sorry for myself, moaning and groaning and wondering why the Lord had let this happen to me.

But this time was different. As I drove home from the doctor's office after getting that report, I was praising the Lord. In effect I said, "Oh, Lord, I thank and praise you for this condition. I know that if it continues in this way I can't last, but I praise you anyway."

And do you know what happened? God turned the situation around and performed a miracle. He took away my appetite for sweets and starches. I can sit down to a meal now with other people gorging themselves on starches and desserts, and I am not the least bit tempted even to sample them.

Ten days after the examination in which I received a bad report, I went back for another blood sugar count. It was normal, and it has been that way ever since. I praised Him, and He met my every need. And He will do the same for you. Try it, and I will guarantee you will believe it.

There is one more thing I want to say about prayer. It is something that I had never thought of until four years ago. At that time I was the speaker for the retreat of pastors of the Baptist General Conference in the Southwest area.

One night during a testimony meeting, a pastor from

Phoenix stood and in effect said, "I have a very small church. For six months about 10 of us were meeting together on a regular basis for prayer. But nothing was happening. Our prayers didn't seem to get any higher than the sound of our voices. It seemed as if Satan would always step in and gain the victory.

"Then we began to think that perhaps we ought to commence our praying by asking God to bind Satan so that he could no longer interfere with our prayer life. We did this and then presented our requests. The answers just poured out. We had a revival; we saw miracles occur." Then he gave illustration after illustration to document the truth of what he was saying.

For example, he told of a young woman who accepted Christ in his church. She was married to a soldier in Vietnam who belonged to a cult that hates evangelical Christianity with a passion. When she wrote him and told him of what she had done, he fired back a letter that should have been written on asbestos. In it he told her in no uncertain terms that he was the head of the house, and that she had to do what he said. He then demanded that she give up her "new religion" and get involved with his cult. He told her that when he returned to the States, she was to go to his meeting house with him every Sunday and there would be no ifs, ands, or buts about it. He was as hard as nails in this matter.

Naturally the wife was heartbroken. She shared the contents of the letter with her pastor and fellow church members. They began to pray about it, asking that God would bind Satan so that he wouldn't be able to influence the husband. They then prayed for the man's salvation.

When the husband came home, God had bound Satan. He didn't even suggest to his wife that she go to his meeting house with him. Instead he attended her church with her. And after several months the Holy Spirit brought him to conviction and conversion. Now the family is complete in Christ Jesus.

Is persistent prayer changing things in your life?

9

Are You a God-glorifier?

2 Thessalonians 1:1-12

Liberal scholars claim that Paul was inconsistent in his teaching of the doctrine of the second coming of Christ. They point out that sometimes he taught that the Lord's return is imminent (that it may come at any moment), while at other times he insisted that certain occurrences must take place before His return. They cite 1 and 2 Thessalonians as exhibit "A" of the contention, stating that 1 Thessalonians indicates an imminent return of Christ while 2 Thessalonians says that certain prophecies must be fulfilled before the Saviour appears.

What they say concerning these books is true, but their criticism is invalid for they fail to harmonize the teaching of the two. Let's look at how they fit together.

In 1 Thessalonians 4:15-18 Paul wrote, "According to the Lord's own word, we tell you that we who are still alive, who are left till the coming of the Lord, will certainly not precede those who have fallen asleep. For the Lord himself will come down from heaven, with a loud command, with the voice of the archangel and with the trumpet call of God, and the dead in Christ will rise first. After that, we who are still alive and are left will be caught up with them in the clouds to meet the Lord in the air. And so we will be with the Lord forever. Therefore encourage each other with these words."

The implication of this passage is that Christ's coming for His own may occur at any moment.

"We ask you, brothers, not to become easily unsettled or alarmed by some prophecy, report or letter supposed to have come from us, saying that the day of the Lord has already come. Don't let anyone deceive you in any way, for that day will not come until the rebellion occurs and the man of lawlessness is revealed, the man doomed to destruction" (2 Thess. 2:1-3).

Here Paul taught that the day of the Lord, which includes the second coming of Christ, will not take place until there is an apostasy in the Church and the Antichrist is revealed.

The question arises, "Are these two passages in conflict?" The answer is an unequivocal *no*. When we look at the two passages carefully, we discover that Paul was not speaking about the same event in these two books.

In 1 Thessalonians he was not referring to the Second Coming; instead he was speaking of the rapture of the Church. You will note in this passage that Christ does not touch the earth; instead both the resurrected and the transformed redeemed are translated to meet Him in the air. In 2 Thessalonians he was referring to Christ's second coming when He returns to establish His earthly kingdom.

You see, our Lord's return, His *parousia,* is presented in two parts in the Scripture; the first part is the rapture, and the last part is the Second Coming. First Thessalonians presents the first part and 2 Thessalonians the last. These two books are in perfect harmony as far as our Lord's return is concerned. The two taken together present the full story of the Second Coming. Please keep this in mind as we study 2 Thessalonians, for Paul had much to say concerning the second advent in this book.

Greetings and Thanks

The great apostle began this epistle with his usual greeting to the church in 2 Thessalonians 1:1,2. Paul, in referring to the Saviour in these two verses, twice called Him, "The Lord Jesus Christ." The word "Jesus," our Saviour's given name, actually means "God is salvation." The word "Christ" is the Greek translation of the Hebrew word for Messiah. In referring to Him in this way Paul was saying that Jesus, who was provided to be salvation for man, is the Messiah of Israel, fulfilling all the Messianic prophecies of the Old Testament, and He is the Lord of the Christian's life.

In verses 3 and 4 Paul pointed out that he was especially thankful for the Thessalonian church, and he gave three reasons for this: first, the people were growing in their faith exceedingly; second, their love one for another was abounding; and third, they persevered and remained faithful in the face of persecution. This church not only was a source of thanksgiving to Paul, but it truly pleased God.

Notice the way Paul introduced the three characteristics of the Thessalonian church. "We ought always to thank God for you, brothers, and rightly so" (v. 3). This is a much stronger statement in the original language than it appears to be in our English translation. There are three words in it that bring this to light.

The first is "ought." This is the translation of *opheilo* which basically means "to owe money, to be in debt"; it can also mean, "bound by duty or necessity to do something."

The second word is "always"; it is the Greek word *panote*. In using it Paul was saying that he was under obligation never to miss a chance to tell the story of the church in Thessalonica.

The third word is "rightly" which is a translation of *apsion*, meaning "befitting, worthy, right."

When we put this all together, we discover that in effect Paul was saying, "Because of your development as a Christ-centered church, I have a sacred obligation to share your story with others every time I have the opportunity; for you are surely worthy of my doing this." And the inference is, "God will use my telling of your story to inspire other churches to become what God wants them to be."

I remember talking to a father who was telling me of his seven-year-old boy. He was as proud as a peacock. Paul was like that father as far as the Thessalonian church was concerned. The Holy Spirit had used him to organize it; he was its first pastor and teacher. Naturally he was excited and thrilled by its development. He was willing and ready to shout its virtues from the housetops.

Every Christian should have this attitude toward his church. He should be willing and eager to share its virtues with others, and he should never criticize or downgrade it. If your church doesn't measure up to your expectations spiritually, before you verbally castigate it, look in the mirror of God's Word to see if you measure up to His expectations spiritually. Bear in mind that you are the church. The corporate organism cannot be any stronger spiritually than you are individually. It just may be that you and people like you are the cause of its coming short of God's standards. If this is the case, it is obvious where your responsibility lies. You must first get yourself straightened out. Then the Holy Spirit will lead you step by step in assisting your church to become what God wants it to be.

Now let us examine the three characteristics of the Thessalonian church that caused Paul to be excited about it and made it a church that pleased the Almighty.

Growing in Faith

First, the people in that church were *growing in their faith* exceedingly. Paul writes in verse 3: " . . . your faith is growing more and more." The words "growing more and more" are a translation of the Greek verb *huperaux-inei* which can also be translated, "to increase beyond measure." This is the only place in the New Testament where this word is used. It is in the present tense, indicating continuous action. This is quite a compliment Paul paid the church. In effect he said, "Your faith is continuously growing; there seems to be no stopping to it; it is already beyond my ability to describe."

The word "faith" as it is used here is not saving faith; instead it is faith that subscribes to the idea that with God nothing shall be impossible. It is faith that motivated David the shepherd boy, when facing Goliath the giant, to say, "This day the Lord will hand you over to me" (1 Sam. 17:46).

In 1 Corinthians 12 a list of the gifts of the Holy Spirit is given. Third in that list is the gift of faith. I am convinced that the Spirit has given this gift to every church. To the measure that church exercises this gift, to that measure God blesses it. The church in Thessalonica exercised that gift to the full and as the result it stands as one of the greatest of the New Testament churches.

One of the great tragedies of present-day American Christianity is the fact that there are many evangelical churches that are sound in doctrine but that are dying on the vine. And the reason? They are not willing to step out and do anything for God unless they are sure that they have more than enough financial backing. Their theory is not "In God we trust" but "In greenbacks we trust," and they are not making it.

The churches that are really moving ahead today are like the Thessalonian church. When they see a need that should be met in the name of Jesus Christ, they step out on faith and meet that need, whether they have the money or not.

In Romans 12:3 Paul wrote, "For by the grace given me I say to every one of you: Do not think of yourself more highly than you ought, but rather think of yourself with sober judgment, in accordance with the measure of faith God has given you." *The Living Bible* translates the last part, " . . . measuring your value by how much faith God has given you." Here is something we must not miss. Our value to Almighty God is indicated by the amount of faith we have and exercise. Or to put it another way: The truly valuable person in God's sight is the one who has, and exercises, unlimited faith in serving Him.

Abounding in Love

Second, Paul was thankful for the Thessalonian church because the members of that church were increasing in their love one for another. Paul used a picture word suggesting the idea of water flooding into a field in abundance so that the crops are all properly irrigated. The Christians who made up the membership of that church literally flooded one another with their love. Visitors coming into their services could sense it; it was warm and magnetic; it drew them to Jesus Christ. Is it any wonder this Thessalonian church was pleasing to God?

100

In 1 Corinthians 12, after the discussion of the gifts of the Spirit, Paul concluded the chapter with these words: "And now I will show you the most excellent way." He then went on in chapter 13 to describe that way, which is the way of love. In that description he told us that "Love is patient, love is kind. It does not envy, it does not boast, it is not proud. It is not rude, it is not self-seeking, it is not easily angered, it keeps no record of wrongs. Love does not delight in evil but rejoices with the truth. It always protects, always trusts, always hopes, always perseveres" (vv. 4-7).

The members of the Thessalonian church walked this way of love; they personified these characteristics of it. Do you? Above everything else today people need and want love.

Once there was a 10-year-old, redheaded, freckle-faced boy who had lived in an orphanage all of his life. His name was Tom. When people came to look over the children for adoption they always turned him down. Then one day a wealthy couple came to the orphanage in their chauffeur-driven Cadillac; she was dressed in mink and satin and he in an expensive hand-tailored suit. They wanted to adopt Tom. As the boy talked to them about it he said, "If you have nothing to offer except a good home, clothes, toys, and the other things most kids have—why, then, I would just as soon stay here."

The wife, quite visibly startled, gasped, "What on earth do you want besides those things that you mention?"

The spunky redhead replied, "I want someone to love me."

All of us are like that little boy! Above everything else we want our fellow Christians to love us. When they do, it makes it easy for us to respond in kind. This pleases the

Lord and is of great assistance in building the church.

Christian, do you really love your fellow Christians? Jesus said, "All men will know that you are my disciples if you love one another" (John 13:35). Are you truly a disciple of Christ or do you just pretend to be? How much love do you have for your fellow Christians?

Remaining Faithful

Third, Paul was grateful for the Thessalonian church because they persevered and remained faithful in the face of persecution. As we turn to Acts 17:1-9 we discover that before Paul got out of town after organizing the church in Thessalonica, a severe persecution was launched against the Christians. Even though this continued without any letup, those believers persevered in serving the Saviour; they met and overcame the test of fire.

Look at the way Paul expressed this in 2 Thessalonians 1:4: "Therefore, among God's churches we boast about your perseverance and faith in all the persecutions and trials you are enduring." In effect the apostle was saying here: "Wherever I go in my missionary travels, I use your church as an illustration of how Christians should respond to persecution and tribulation. You are a perfect example of what God expects the church to be when confronted with diabolical opposition. Instead of giving in to it, you just keep on keeping on doing your thing for God."

I saw a modern example of this back in 1966 when I attended the First Baptist Church in Moscow one Sunday night. I was greatly impressed by the fact that there were about 300 teenagers there. During the benediction I peeked. Since they were sitting across the balcony from me I was able to look into their eyes, and as I did I noticed that most of them were crying.

After the service I asked my 19-year-old interpreter why this was. She replied, "They were weeping because they are so happy in the Lord."

I then queried, "Do they pay a price for being Christians?"

Her answer chilled me. She said, "If they are straight A students, no; but if they are less than that, they are made to drop out of school, and their future is bleak. The boys are destined to be street sweepers and garbage collectors, while the girls will be chambermaids." And then she added, "They gladly pay this price, refusing to give up their faith because of their love for Jesus." You talk about perseverance and remaining faithful! That's really it!

In our land, however, the only opposition we face in serving Jesus is discouragement. And the tragedy of this is that the majority of Christians give in to it. Instead of persevering in their service for the King of kings, they quit.

The Thessalonian Christians pleased God because they refused to quit. What about you? Are you sitting on the sidelines, nursing your wounds and feeling sorry for yourself, or are you out on the battlefield for God? Are you a quitter or a perseverer?

Eternal Consequences

One of the most assuring promises that God gives to the Christian who has to suffer for his faith is found in Romans 12:19: "Do not take revenge, my friends, but leave room for God's wrath, for it is written: 'It is mine to avenge; I will repay,' says the Lord." In 2 Thessalonians 1:5-10 Paul enlarged on this idea, discussing it in detail. In so doing he took the long look, measuring the Christian's life not only in terms of time but eternity.

A careful analysis of this passage reveals that it can be

103

outlined in terms of three important considerations: (1) A description of what Christ will ultimately do with the enemies of righteousness; (2) A threefold message addressed to the suffering saints in Thessalonica; (3) Paul's prayer requests for the Thessalonians and for all Christians.

The Enemies of Righteousness

First, Paul described what Christ will ultimately do with the enemies of righteousness. Notice in the last part of 2 Thessalonians 1:8 that he referred to these people as those who "do not know God and do not obey the gospel of our Lord Jesus."

The gospel is the good news of salvation that God has provided for all men through the death, burial, and resurrection of our Lord Jesus Christ. To obey the gospel means to accept it by faith, trusting Jesus Christ as Saviour and Lord. Those who do not obey the gospel are those who reject Christ. In other words, all Christ rejecters are enemies of righteousness; they are enemies of God, and if they continue in that way they will be the objects of His wrath.

Many people don't understand this. They have the idea that the gospel is a take-it-or-leave-it proposition. If we can judge by their actions, they feel that the important things in life are clothes, cars, homes, money, and fun. But this is as far from the truth as the east is from the west.

You are either a friend of God or an enemy of God, depending on whether or not you obey the gospel. You can be a member of the best service club in the community and still be an enemy of God; you can serve on the board of any number of charitable organizations and still be an enemy of God.

If you are an enemy of God and still persist in following

this course of action, Paul spelled out exactly what is going to happen to you. Consider carefully his words: "and give relief to you who are troubled, and to us as well. This will happen when the Lord Jesus is revealed from heaven in blazing fire with his powerful angels. He will punish those who do not know God and do not obey the gospel of our Lord Jesus. They will be punished with everlasting destruction and shut out from the presence of the Lord and from the majesty of his power on the day he comes to be glorified in his holy people and to be marveled at among all those who have believed. This includes you, because you believed our testimony to you" (2 Thess. 1:7-10).

In these verses Paul called to our attention two important considerations: the second coming of Christ, and His administration of justice when He comes.

Notice the way in which Paul pictured the second coming of Christ: "When the Lord Jesus is revealed . . . " (v. 7). The word "revealed" is *apokolupsei,* meaning "to be unveiled." Even though Christ is hidden from our sight now, there is a moment coming in the future when He shall be unveiled to be seen by all.

Paul went on to inform us that He will come with "powerful angels" or the angels of His power (v. 7). Keep this in mind.

Paul described Christ as coming "in blazing fire," (v. 7) or a more accurate translation, "in a fire of flame." Dr. Edmond Hiebert, commenting on this, points out that "The Old Testament theophanies were frequently marked by the presence of fire speaking of the divine majesty and indignation against sin. This Old Testament concept of the fiery manifestation of Jehovah's presence is now ascribed to the returning Lord Jesus. It is . . . testimony to the true deity of Jesus Christ."[1]

His return will be a glorious sight for His friends, those who have been converted during the tribulation period. Verse 10 informs us that when He comes He will be glorified in His saints and marveled at by all those who believe in Him.

Verses 7-10 also inform us that He is going to administer justice to those who have rejected Him and consequently have made themselves His enemies. Notice carefully the words of verses 8,9. When He comes He is going to take vengeance on His enemies by punishing them with everlasting destruction from the presence of the Lord and from the glory of His power.

As we look at this there are three facts that must be considered.

Fact number one has to do with "his powerful angels" who accompany Him when He comes again. In our Lord's parable of the wheat and tares (see Matt. 13:24-30), He tells about a farmer who sows good seed in his farm. While he and his men are asleep one night an enemy slips in and sows tares among the wheat.

As the crops begin to develop the farmer's men discover that both wheat and tares are growing together. They want to go out and pull up the tares immediately. But the farmer forbids it, for fear that they also might pull up some of the wheat. He tells them that both crops will grow until the harvest. Then they will have the reapers gather the tares into bundles and burn them up before the reaping of the wheat.

There is no guesswork connected with the interpretation of this parable. Jesus gives it to us in Matthew 13:37-43: "The one who sowed the good seed is the Son of Man. The field is the world, and the good seed stands for the sons of the kingdom. The weeds are the sons of the evil one, and the enemy who sows them is the devil. The harvest is the end of the age, and the harvesters are angels. As the weeds are pulled up and burned in the fire, so it will be at the end of the age. The Son of Man will send out his angels, and they will weed out of his kingdom everything that causes sin and all who do evil. They will throw them into the fiery furnace, where there will be weeping and gnashing of teeth. Then the righteous will shine like the sun in the kingdom of their Father. He who has ears, let him hear."

What a frightening, nightmarish picture this is for those who are enemies of God, for those who are Christ rejecters. Here we are told that the first thing the conquering Saviour is going to do when He returns is have the angels of His power who accompany Him gather His enemies together and destroy them with fire.

Fact number two: following the millennial period, God's enemies will be raised to face Christ at the judgment of the great white throne which is described in Revelation 20:11-15. There they will be given the sentence indicated by 2 Thessalonians 1:9.

Fact number three takes us back to verse 6. There Paul wrote, "God is just: He will pay back trouble to those who trouble you." Here the great apostle was pointing out that the Lord Jesus Christ is perfectly justified in banishing those who reject Him, both from the eternal presence of God and from the presence of their believing loved ones. You ask why is this? The answer is clear.

If you are an enemy of God, a Christ rejecter, the Saviour is constantly holding out His arms of redeeming love to you. He is inviting you to get your values and priorities straightened out. He is urging you to receive by faith His gift of eternal life. If you persist in turning your back upon this love, either until you go into a Christless grave or until He comes again, you leave Him no alternative. Justice demands your everlasting punishment. You will get what you deserve. The choice is left up to you. You can either receive His mercy by faith or His justice in eternity.

A Message for Suffering Saints

In verse 5 and in the first part of verse 7 Paul addressed a threefold message to the persecuted saints in Thessalonica and through them a message to all Christians who suffer for their faith. Strange as it may seem, we have people in this category in the United States. Their suffering basically is not physical, but mental and psychological.

Many Christian young people have parents who make their lives miserable because they are Christians. These moms and dads go out of their way to prevent them from attending the services. They criticize them; they laugh at them; they scorn them; and some go even so far as to offer to raise their allowances if they will renounce Jesus Christ. They use every brainwashing technique they know in order to separate their kids from their Christian faith. These persecuted young people are included in Paul's message to the Thessalonians.

The first part of the message is found in the first statement in verse 5: "All this is evidence that God's judgment is right." The words, "All this" refer to the last part of verse 4 where we are told that the Thessalonians were suffering persecutions and tribulations. The phrase, "that God's judgment is right," refers to the judgment that Christ is going to pour out on the enemies of righteousness when He comes again.

Paul was saying, "The persecutions and tribulations that you Thessalonian Christians are now experiencing are

108

a plain indication—proof positive—that the judgment that Christ is going to rain down on your persecutors is a righteous judgment; it is no more severe than they deserve."

The second part of the message in verse 5 is: "as a result you will be counted worthy of the kingdom of God, for which you are suffering." In effect Paul was saying, "From man's point of view you prove your worthiness of the Kingdom of God by being willing to sacrifice and suffer for it."

Notice that I said, "From man's point of view." From God's point of view the Christian is counted worthy of His Kingdom through the death, burial, and resurrection of the Saviour. But when the believer suffers and sacrifices for Jesus he proves to other people the sincerity of his profession of faith and he demonstrates his worthiness as a Christian. This is the most powerful magnet the Holy Spirit has in drawing others to Christ.

The third part of Paul's message to the persecuted Christians is found in verse 7: "And so I would say to you who are suffering, God will give you rest along with us when the Lord Jesus appears suddenly from heaven in flaming fire with his mighty angels" *(TLB)*.

Here we find Paul taking the long look as far as the Christians are concerned. In so doing he assured us that we are not always going to have to suffer for our faith. When Christ comes again He is going to deliver His own from their tormentors. He will give us eternal peace, rest, and relaxation in that place called heaven which He has prepared for us. John, the beloved, in describing this place in Revelation 21:4, pictures it as a land of no tears: "He will wipe every tear from their eyes. There will be no more death or mourning or crying or pain, for the old order of things has passed away."

109

Paul's Prayer Requests

Finally Paul shared his prayer requests for the Thessalonians and for all Christians. He wrote: "With this in mind, we constantly pray for you, that our God may count you worthy of his calling, and that by his power he may fulfill every good purpose of yours and every act prompted by your faith. We pray this so that the name of our Lord Jesus may be glorified in you, and you in him, according to the grace of our God and the Lord Jesus Christ" (2 Thess. 1:11,12).

If you will look carefully at verse 11 you will discover that in it Paul listed three prayer requests that build one on the other.

First, he prayed that God would count, or make them worthy of His calling. This is just another way of praying that Christians might be filled with the Holy Spirit. No one can possibly be worthy of the call of the Almighty to serve Him unless he allows the Spirit of God to control his life.

The second prayer request builds on the first. *The Living Bible* translates this prayer request: "That our God . . . will make you as good as you wish you could be!" Another way to say it is, "that God will enable all Christians to live above the line of compromise." Only as we do this will our testimonies be of any value, for a compromising Christian is one of the greatest assets the devil has.

A sign on a church billboard read, "A moderately good Christian is like a moderately good egg." Not very appetizing! We must live without compromise. And the only way we can do this is to allow the Spirit of God to control our lives.

Third, Paul prayed for the Thessalonians and all Christians that God would enable them and us to engage in a work of faith characterized by power. Charles Haddon

Spurgeon said, "O brethren, be great believers! Little faith will bring your souls to heaven, but great faith will bring heaven to your soul." People of great accomplishment for God are those who are willing to step out on faith, believing that the Almighty will enable them to complete that which He has called them to do. An anonymous writer has put it this way: "If there should arise one utterly believing man, the history of the world might be changed."

In verse 12 Paul concluded this section by stating why he made these three prayer requests. "Then everyone will be praising the name of the Lord Jesus Christ because of the results they see in you; and your greatest glory will be that you belong to him. The tender mercy of our God and of the Lord Jesus Christ has made all this possible for you" *(TLB)*.

Are people praising the Lord Jesus Christ because you are filled with the Spirit, because you are living above the line of compromise, and because you are accomplishing by faith great things for God?

Footnote
1. Edmond Hiebert, *The Thessalonian Epistles: A Call to Readiness* (Chicago: Moody Press, 1971), p. 289.

10
I Know Who Holds the Future

2 Thessalonians 2:1-17

If a group of competent Bible scholars were commissioned to make a list of the most significant prophetic sections in the Word of God, you can rest assured, that high on that list would be 2 Thessalonians 2:1-12.

As we peruse this passage carefully we discover that in it Paul is pointing out four significant truths: (1) the Thessalonian Christians were being victimized by false teachers who did not understand prophecy; (2) the coming of the day of the Lord will be marked by two major events; (3) the coming Antichrist is a very unsavory character; (4) the Temple in Jerusalem has to be rebuilt before Christ returns to earth.

False Teachers

Paul calls attention to the fact that the Thessalonian Christians were being victimized by false teachers who did not understand prophecy. Evidently some people had come into their group who had professed that they were led by the Spirit and that they had a letter from Paul stating that the day of the Lord had already commenced. In other words, the rapture had already occurred and they had missed it, and within a short time they could expect to experience a period of great tribulation.

Naturally they were upset by this. Paul appeals to them to calm down: "Concerning the coming of our Lord Jesus Christ and our being gathered to him, we ask you, brothers, not to become easily unsettled or alarmed by some prophecy, report or letter supposed to have come from us, saying that the day of the Lord has already come" (vv. 1, 2). The significant word in verse 2 is the verb "unsettled"; it is a Greek word *saleuthanai*, which denotes a rocking motion, a shaking up and down, like a building shaken by an earthquake or a ship tossed by the sea. The verb is in the past tense, indicating that the shaking comes from without. The Thessalonian Christians were being intellectually and spiritually rocked by the false teachers who had come to them, and Paul was concerned about it. By implication, he told them to let the teachings of these people go in one ear and out the other. Their doctrine of the day of the Lord was completely false.

We need to heed this same plea of Paul's. We have a similar situation confronting us today. The Jehovah's Witnesses are sending out their missionaries two by two into our homes and into our places of business, telling us that Christ has already come back. They have their own translation of the Bible which has been manipulated to substantiate their false teaching. With smiles on their faces they graciously offer to conduct Bible classes in our homes. And the tragedy of this is that myriads of people are falling into their trap by accepting their proposal.

You ask, "What are the results?" Most of the members

in this group are former Baptists, Methodists, Pentecostals, Nazarenes, Presbyterians, Lutherans, Episcopalians, and so on—people who did not study their Bibles while they were in their former churches. Consequently, not only are they now spiritually blind, but they are in bondage to a satanic cult whose design is to think for them, direct them, and make all of their decisions for them.

Many other people who were formerly in this cult have truly been converted to Jesus Christ, whom they recognize to be co-equal with the Father and the Holy Spirit. They know that His coming is in the future. When one of them is asked to give his testimony, he will often say, "I am free! I am free! I am free!" That is what Paul wanted for the Thessalonian Christians and that is what God wants for all people—to be truly free in Christ, looking forward to that day when He comes again.

Two Major Events

Second, Paul called to our attention that the coming of the day of the Lord will be marked by two major events: "Don't let anyone deceive you in any way, for that day will not come until the rebellion occurs and the man of lawlessness is revealed, the man doomed to destruction" (v. 3).

The first thing that must take place before the day of the Lord is what Paul called the apostasy. According to W.E. Vine's *Expository Dictionary of New Testament Words,* it literally means "a defection," "a revolt."[1] In commenting on the significance of this word, D. Edmond Hiebert writes, "The falling away indicates a tragic movement within the sphere of professed Christendom, the treason of the avowed friends of Christ . . . it denotes a deliberate abandonment of a formerly professed position or view, a defection, a rejection of a former allegiance."[2]

115

In other words, what Paul is saying here in using "apostasy" is that, as the time approaches for the end of this age and the beginning of the day of the Lord, there is going to be a turning away from Jesus and the fundamentals of the faith on the part of those who have professed to love Him and trust Him as Saviour. Christianity is going to become more and more a minority movement.

Jesus Himself recognized this and taught it. When He concluded telling the parable of the importunate woman, He raised this question: "When the Son of Man comes, will he find faith on the earth?" (Luke 18:8).

And without trying to set any dates let me say that we are seeing this apostasy taking place, and it is growing in momentum. Thirty-five years ago the whole world looked upon the United States as a Christian nation. But this is not true today. The majority of people in the United States have turned their backs on Jesus Christ; they live as if He never existed and has no claim upon their lives. And to add insult to injury, many of these have their names on the membership rolls of evangelical churches.

Another evidence of apostasy today is seen in the preaching that comes from many Protestant pulpits. Sociology is substituted for theology; Freudian psychology rather than Jesus Christ is held up as man's Saviour and the answer to his problems; political activism rather than witnessing is propounded as the need of the hour. The Bible is not even on the preferred reading list. People in these churches don't have the foggiest notion of how to be saved or what it means to be saved. They are the spiritually blind being led by those who are spiritually blind.

This trend will increase and intensify until "the day of the Lord" begins, and then it will get worse.

The second event that must take place before "the day

116

of the Lord" is the revelation of the "man of lawlessness," the Antichrist. As a matter of fact, he is revealed as the day of the Lord begins. When will that be?

Paul answered this question in verses 6-8. "And you know what is keeping him from being here already; for he can come only when his time is ready. As for the work this man of rebellion and hell will do when he comes, it is already going on, but he himself will not come until the one who is holding him back steps out of the way. Then this wicked one will appear" *(TLB)*.

Here Paul set forth two very important truths: First, there is One in the world who is holding evil back, keeping it from taking complete control of man. Second, when this One is removed from the earth, then the Antichrist will be revealed. The question immediately arises, "Who is this One?"

Through the years many and varied have been the answers. Some have suggested that it is Paul; others have claimed that it is the succession of the Roman emperors; still others have argued that it is the Roman Empire, the embodiment of law and order. Some have even contended that it is Satan himself, which puts him out of character, to say the least. Obviously, none of these answers is correct.

Who is this One? There can be only one possible answer—the Holy Spirit. Jesus said that when He came He would convict the world of sin. This He has been doing through the Church ever since Pentecost; and this He will continue to do until He is taken out of the world. And when He goes, so will the Church go, for He is now indwelling every believer (see John 14:17). In other words, the Holy Spirit will be removed at the rapture of the Church, and then the Antichrist will be revealed and the day of the Lord will begin.

117

The Antichrist

Third, Paul pointed out that the Antichrist is a very unsavory character; he is not one who will bear close acquaintance, and he is surely not one to be desired as a close personal friend. Second Thessalonians 2:3-12 give six facts concerning him.

First, he is the man of lawlessness (see v. 3). This simply means that he is devoted to the cause of sin; all of the supernatural power which the devil will give him will be devoted to the fostering and promotion of sin in its most heinous forms.

Second, he is a blasphemer. How graphically verse 4 calls this to our attention: "He opposes and exalts himself over everything that is called God or is worshiped, and even sets himself up in God's temple, proclaiming himself to be God." And then in verse 5 Paul reminded the Thessalonians that he had told them this when he had been with them the first time.

Third, he is the lawless one. In verse 8 we read, "Then the lawless one will be revealed." The word translated "lawless" is *anomos*—it is made up of two words, *a* meaning "no" and *nomos* meaning "law." He will be a man who will recognize no law but his own.

Fourth, He is an imitator of Christ. He will come with all power, counterfeit miracles, signs and wonders (see v. 9). "Signs and wonders" are the very terms that are used to describe the miracles that Christ performed. Just as Jesus substantiated His claims as the Son of God by the performing of miracles, so the Antichrist will do the same. And it will be Satan who will bestow upon him this supernatural power. In the first part of verse 9 we are told that his coming is in accordance with the working of Satan.

Fifth, he is a deceiver. "And in every sort of evil that

deceives those who are perishing. They perish because they refused to love the truth and so be saved" (v. 10). The Antichrist is going to deceive many into believing that he really is the Christ. And for this they will pay a terrible price. "So God will allow them to believe lies with all their hearts, and all of them will be justly judged for believing falsehood, refusing the Truth, and enjoying their sins" (vv. 11,12, *TLB*).

Sixth, he is doomed to destruction. This is emphasized in verses 3 and 8. In verse 3 he is referred to as the man doomed to "destruction," destruction not in the sense of extinction, but in the sense of a loss of well-being. This will be the experience of all who spend eternity in hell.

In verse 8 we are told that the Lord will overthrow him with the breath of His mouth and shall destroy him by the splendor of His coming. The Antichrist won't stand a chance when he meets the real Christ at the final battle of Armageddon. Revelation 19:20 says the Saviour will cast him into the lake of fire burning with brimstone.

One important point: no Christian in our day has to worry about the Antichrist. Why? Because those of us who belong to Christ will take part in the rapture which precedes his reign of terror. People who are converted during the tribulation period will have to be concerned with him, but not those of us who turn to Christ now.

The Temple Rebuilt

Fourth, Paul called to our attention that the Temple in Jerusalem must be rebuilt before Christ returns to the earth. During the tribulation period the Antichrist will set himself up as God in the Temple of God and demand that people worship him (see v. 4). For him to be able to do this, it is axiomatic that there has to be a Temple.

A new Temple could not have been constructed prior to the Six Day War in 1967. Before that war the Temple area, which is located on Mount Moriah where Abraham offered Isaac as a sacrifice, was in the hands of the Jordanians. But when Israel defeated the Arabs in 1967 the Jewish soldiers raced through the narrow winding streets of the Old City and rushed up to kiss their Wailing Wall. Moshe Dayan, the commander of the armed forces, summed up the feelings of all Israel when he said, "We've returned to our holiest of holy places, never to leave it again."[3]

Even though the Mosque of Omar is situated on that site now, the day will come when the Moslems will be completely eliminated from that place, the mosque torn down, and a new Temple built there. You can be sure that when the time comes for this to be done, it will be announced to every Jewish community in the world, and more than enough will be sent in to accomplish this feat.

Immediately after the Six Day War, one of the editors of *Time* magazine interviewed the famous Jewish historian, Israel Eldad. When he was asked about the possibility of rebuilding the Temple in Jerusalem, he replied, "When the Jewish people took over Jerusalem the first time, under King David, only one generation passed before they built the temple, and so shall it be with us."

When asked about the problem of the Dome of the Rock being on the Jewish Temple site, he replied with a wink, "Who knows, perhaps there will be an earthquake!"[4]

Whether God uses an earthquake or some other means to destroy the Mosque of Omar is of little consequence. He will see to it that it is destroyed and replaced by a new Temple. And this will be done before Christ returns to establish His earthly rule.

Prior to that time He is going to come for His Church. There is no prophecy to be fulfilled before this takes place. If today were God's appointed moment for His return, would you be ready? Can you truly pray as did John the apostle, "Even so, come, Lord Jesus" (Rev. 22:20, *KJV*)?

Paul's Thanksgiving for the Thessalonians

Paul began verse 13 with the little word, "but," which is a conjunction; it joins that which goes before with that which follows. In this section of God's Word it is most significant because it highlights a tremendously important contrast.

In 2 Thessalonians 2:1-12, Paul opened a window to the future, allowing us to see something of that which is going to transpire during the tribulation. He gave us a graphic picture of the destruction of the Antichrist and those who allow themselves to be fooled by him.

But then Paul wrote, "But we ought always to thank God for you, brothers loved by the Lord, because from the beginning God chose you to be saved through the sanctifying work of the Spirit and through belief in the truth. He called you to this through our gospel, that you might share in the glory of our Lord Jesus Christ" (vv. 13,14). Do you see the contrast here? Whereas the Christ-rejecters described in verses 8-12 are doomed, those who receive Christ are forever saved.

The truth that this contrast emphasizes is the fact that from God's vantage point there are only two types of people in the world: Christ-rejecters or Christ-receivers. Categories such as rich or poor, white or black, popular or unpopular have absolutely no significance in God's sight. You are either a Christ-rejecter or a Christ-receiver, and you determine which.

In expressing his gratitude for the Thessalonian Christ-receivers Paul calls to our attention four basic facts of Christianity.

First, God chooses the believer for Himself (see v. 13). What a beautiful and significant concept this is. Just think of it. God from the very beginning of time once and for all chose each Christian for Himself, that we may enter into a never-ending love relationship with Him who is our Creator.

The most satisfying and at the same time the most intriguing relationship in the world is a love relationship. Jonathan and David had such a relationship, but it ended with the death of Jonathan. Robert Browning and Elizabeth Barrett Browning had such a relationship, but it ended with Elizabeth's demise.

The love relationship that we have through Christ with our heavenly Father gets better all the time. It is like the words of the old hymn, "Sweeter As the Years Go By." And it doesn't end in death; it goes on and on through all of eternity. Aren't you glad that God chose you for Himself?

Second, God, not man, does the choosing. The words of Scripture are very plain and forthright at this point. Now it seems to me I can just see you thinking something like this to yourself: "This is not fair. God, according to Paul's teaching here, has His pets, those whom He chooses to be saved, while allowing all others to go to hell. He is surely an arbitrary Being."

Let me urge you not to get your exercise by jumping to conclusions. Reserve your judgment until you consider the remaining facts which Paul emphasized here.

Third, God does the choosing through the presentation of the gospel (see v. 14). I like the way *The Living Bible* puts this: "Through us he told you the Good News.

122

Through us he called you to share in the glory of our Lord Jesus Christ." Here Paul is simply emphasizing that God calls people to salvation through the preaching of the gospel.

Before this picture is complete, however, there are two other verses we must consider. The first is Mark 16:15, "Go into all the world and preach the good news to all creation." The second is 1 Timothy 2:4; in speaking about God, Paul here writes, "Who wants all men to be saved and to come to a knowledge of the truth."

Whom does God call to be saved? Every creature in all the world. What is His will? That all be saved and come to the knowledge of the truth!

You see, God is not an arbitrary, capricious Being who saves only His pets while predestining all others to go to hell. Instead, His call is universal to every man, woman, and child. All are chosen by Him for salvation. But not all are saved! You ask why? Because they, themselves, turn their backs on God. Their lostness is not the fault of our heavenly Father! They have only themselves to blame.

Fourth, the individual becomes numbered among the chosen of God—the saved—through belief in the truth and the sanctification of the Spirit (see 2 Thess. 2:13). "The truth" referred to here is Jesus Christ who said "I am . . . the truth" (John 14:6).

The work of the Holy Spirit in sanctifying a person is that of purifying him and setting him apart to serve the Saviour. What Paul is saying here is the central core of Christian truth. It may be paraphrased like this: "When a person through the Holy Spirit, in response to the call of the Father, puts his faith in Jesus Christ as the Truth, the Spirit then purifies him and indwells him so that he can serve the Lord Jesus Christ effectively."

In commenting on the Spirit's indwelling and sanctifying ministry in the life of the believer, Paul pointed out a most assuring truth: "Being confident of this, that he who began a good work in you will carry it on to completion until the day of Jesus Christ" (Phil. 1:6).

The reason so many Christians are unhappy and frustrated today is that they have not turned the controls of their lives over to the Holy Spirit. It is impossible for a believer to be anything but happy and excited about Jesus when the Holy Spirit is at the helm of his life.

Paul's Exhortation to the Thessalonians

In verse 15 Paul exhorted the Thessalonians, "So then, brothers, stand firm and hold to the teachings we passed on to you, whether by word of mouth or by letter." The phrase "so then" connects this exhortation with that which has gone before. In using it Paul was saying, "Because of what God has done for you in providing salvation, security, sanctification and an opportunity for service, I exhort you to stand fast and hold the teachings which you have been taught, whether by word or our epistle."

The word "teaching" comes from the Greek *paradosis*, and it literally means, "that which is transmitted or passed on." It pictures a teacher communicating truth to his pupil. Paul had been their teacher. While he was with them he had interpreted the Old Testament for them in the light of Jesus Christ. After leaving he had written them a letter, 1 Thessalonians, to which he referred in this verse. It was his desire that the Thessalonian Christians take an unequivocal stand for the truths which he had shared with them both orally and in writing.

God honors both Christians and churches that take an

unequivocal stand for His Word. This is what Paul exhorted the Thessalonians to do.

Paul's Prayer for the Thessalonians

Paul prayed for the Thessalonian Christians. "May our Lord Jesus Christ himself and God our Father, who loved us and by his grace gave us eternal encouragement and good hope, encourage your hearts and strengthen you in every good deed and word" (vv. 16,17).

A careful analysis of this prayer reveals that Paul was making two requests for the Thessalonian Christians.

First, he was requesting that God would comfort them. The word translated "encourage" is the verb *parakalesai* which is made up of two words, *para* meaning "for," and *kaleo,* meaning "to call." From this verbal form we get the noun *paraklatos* or "paraclete"; it means "one called or sent for to assist another"; "one present to render beneficial service." This is one of the names Jesus used in referring to the Holy Spirit. In John 14:16 Jesus promised His disciples, "And I will pray the Father, and he shall give you another Comforter" *(KJV)*. Here he was referring to the Holy Spirit as the promised One who would come upon them to assist them, and to render beneficial services to them.

All of this is implied in Paul's prayer that God would comfort or encourage the Thessalonian Christians. You see, they were constantly under the gun of persecution. There must have been times when they were so discouraged that they were ready to call it quits. The great apostle was aware of this. He therefore prayed that they would constantly allow the Spirit of God to buoy them up, to encourage them, to meet their need.

This prayer should be on the lips of every Christian for

fellow Christians who are facing what appears to be insur-mountable difficulties.

The second request in Paul's prayer for the Thessalonians is closely akin to the first. In it he importuned God that He would strengthen them in every good word and work. The verb "strengthen" is a translation of *sterizo;* it means "to stand immovable." Here Paul was asking God to enable his Christian friends in Thessalonica to stand immovable in the face of hostility and persecution, both in what they had to say about Jesus and in the way they worked for Him.

Because of the freedom that we enjoy in America, this prayer doesn't mean much to us in terms of our own experience. However, it does in nations such as the Soviet Union. Those who are dedicated to Christ there are constantly being harassed; the State is out to get them by fair means and foul. They face economic privation, imprisonment, incarceration in insane asylums, and even martyrdom.

Through the years, however, there have been and there are faithful Christians praying for their Russian brothers and sisters in Christ. One of their prayers is that God would give them the strength to take an unequivocal stand for Christ; that He would enable them to remain immovable both in what they have to say about Jesus and in their work for Him.

These prayers are being answered. David Benson in his book, *Miracle in Moscow,* tells about Basil, whom he has come to know, during his many visits to the Soviet Union, as a beloved Christian brother.

One evening as David was talking to him, Basil said, "I lost my job today for the third time in six months. I was caught witnessing in the factory at lunch break. This, you know, is a crime. Look at where I am! I have a wife, an infant son and a crippled father-in-law to support. Because I am a Christian I cannot have any kind of insurance or old-age pension. Our family is penniless and I don't know what to do next." Then his face became almost luminous with joy as he said, "From a human point of view everything is hopeless. But as a Christian I have never been more secure."[5]

In a subsequent conversation Basil told David Benson about his preaching to several hundred young people out in the woods.

Suddenly the police broke in on them, and the youth began to run. Basil immediately called them back, telling them that if they ran they would show fear. He pointed out that there was no need for this because they had God's love, which casts out fear.

He then continued his sermon until a soldier interrupted, asking, "What are you doing?"

Calmly Basil responded, "We are singing hymns, praying, and listening to the Word of God; we are not talking about anything political."

He then continued his sermon while the police walked away. You see, he remained immovable both in what he had to say about Jesus and in his service to Him.

There are two lessons in this: First, as Christians it is both our privilege and our responsibility to pray for our Christian brothers and sisters who are facing persecution because of their faith. Our prayer should be the same as that of Paul's for the Thessalonian believers, that God would make them immovable both in speaking about Jesus and in serving Him. And we have the assurance that God will answer. Let us not neglect our suffering brothers and sisters.

Second, we need to see in this the lesson of holy boldness. Basil personified this in his confrontation with the police who had the authority to kill him with no questions asked.

The reason most of us are ineffective in our witnessing for Jesus is that we lack this characteristic. We can talk to our friends about the weather, about sports, and about 101 other subjects, but when it comes to speaking to them about Jesus, we freeze.

God grant that each of us, like Basil, will allow the Holy Spirit to bestow upon us the gift of holy boldness!

Footnotes
1. W.E. Vine, *Expository Dictionary of New Testament Words,* Vol. II (Westwood: Fleming H. Revell Company, 1940), p. 73.
2. Edmond Hiebert, *The Thessalonian Epistles: A Call to Readiness* (Chicago: Moody Press, 1971), p. 305.
3. Hal Lindsay, *There's a New World Coming* (Irvine: Harvest House Publishers, 1973), p. 158.
4. Ibid., p. 159.
5. David Benson, *Miracle in Moscow* (Ventura: Regal Books, 1975), p. 75.

11
The Benefits
of Busyness

2 Thessalonians 3:6-15

We come now to the final chapter of the second Thessalonians epistle, which we will consider in two separate sections. Verses 6-15 of 2 Thessalonians comprise one of the most sobering segments of instruction in both epistles. The content of this section is Paul's straightforward counsel on how to respond to those in the Body of Christ who are undisciplined and lazy. These verses are sandwiched between 2 Thessalonians 3:1-5 and 3:16-18, a collection of final thoughts from the great apostle as he brings the second epistle to a close. We will consider the "meat" portion of the sandwich briefly here, then look at the verses which bookend it in the final chapter.

Paul's Commands

In 2 Thessalonians 3:6-15 Paul issued five commands for the Thessalonian Christians to implement in their lives. The reason for these commands is found in verse 11: "We hear that some among you are idle. They are not busy; they are busybodies."

129

There is more than meets the eye in this verse. Paul was dealing with a live issue related to the second coming of Christ. Some of the Thessalonians were convinced that Christ was going to come at any moment. They therefore refused to work, depending on their Christian neighbors to provide their food for them while they spent their time in idle gossip.

Against this historical backdrop, let me point out the five commands in their logical sequence.

Earn Your Own Bread

The first is recorded in verse 12: "Such people we command and urge in the Lord Jesus Christ to settle down and earn the bread they eat." Paul had the idea that if a person got hungry enough he would work. That is a practical idea!

Avoid Idle Brothers

Paul's third command is stated twice: in verse 6 we read, "In the name of the Lord Jesus Christ, we command you, brothers, to keep away from every brother who is idle and does not live according to the teaching you received from us." And in verse 14 we read, "If anyone does not obey our instruction in this letter, take special note of him. Do not associate with him, in order that he may feel ashamed."

The reason for this command should be obvious. Paul wanted those Christians who were working and providing for their own needs to withdraw from those who refused to do this, so that the non-Christians in that community would recognize that there is sanity in Christianity; that not everyone who professed to be a Christian was a psycho-ceramic (crackpot).

130

Warn and Win

Paul's fourth command is recorded in verse 15: "Yet do not regard him as an enemy, but warn him as a brother." Here Paul was simply saying that the working Christians should not give up on those who refuse to work. Even though they separate themselves from them, they should take every opportunity afforded them to admonish their Christian brothers to get on the ball for God.

Here is a basic principle that we should put into practice. When it becomes necessary for us to separate ourselves from a Christian brother because of some immoral activity in which he is engaged, we should nevertheless maintain some contact with him; so that whenever the opportunity presents itself we can urge him to repent and get right with the Lord. Who knows? The Holy Spirit just might use our words to bring him back into fellowship with the Lord and with his brothers and sisters in Christ.

Meanwhile, Keep Doing Right

Paul's fifth command recorded in verse 13 is written to encourage those who were really making their lives count for Christ. Notice the wording of it: "And as for you, brothers, never tire of doing what is right." The reason for this command is given in Galatians 6:9: "Let us not become weary in doing good, for at the proper time we will reap a harvest if we do not give up." The Christian who just keeps on serving the Saviour will one day stand before the judgment seat of Christ and receive the rewards prepared for the faithful. The Bible does not tell us what these rewards are. But you can be sure that if the Lord has prepared them, they will surely be of infinite value, bringing happiness and satisfaction to those who have them.

131

12
Let's Be Prayer Partners

2 Thessalonians 3:1-5; 16-18

Paul closes his letter to the Thessalonian believers with a series of requests, praises, prayers, commands and commendations.

Paul's Requests

First, Paul shared with the Thessalonians a twofold prayer request that was heavy on his heart. "Finally, brothers, pray for us that the message of the Lord may spread rapidly and be honored, just as it was with you. And pray that we may be delivered from wicked and evil men, for not everyone has faith" (2 Thess. 3:1,2).

The Christians in the first century, like the believers behind the Iron Curtain today, faced almost insurmountable opposition as they sought to spread the good news. Diabolic forces were arrayed on every side against them. The enemies of the cross were willing to lie, cheat, steal and even murder to stop the progress of Christianity, and many of them were so insensitive to truth that they believed that they were doing God a favor by persecuting Christians.

Paul realized that only the power of God Himself was sufficient to gain the victory over them. So he asked the Thessalonians to pray that God by His Spirit would enable the message of Christ to spread rapidly, gaining converts wherever it went, and that He would encircle His servants with His providential care.

God wants us to believe that He answers prayer. In James 4:2 we are told that we do not have because we do not ask.

We are to carry everything to God in prayer. Failure to do so robs us of blessings; for God answers prayer today just as He did in the first century.

A letter written to the editor of a paper published by UTLA, a teachers' union in the city of Los Angeles, reads:

"During Christmas vacation in 1970, vandalism at our school climaxed in gross destruction. Such vandalism continued thereafter over every weekend. There seemed to be no answer to the problem on a human level.

"In the spring of 1970, four of us teachers decided to join together in a weekly prayer meeting, outside of school time, to entreat God, in the name of Jesus, for our school. Little by little the vandalism decreased, until today, there is seldom a break-in. When there is, little or no damage is done, and usually nothing is missing. Our prayer group is continuing, and has increased to seven members."

When we meet the conditions, God fulfills His promises. Yes, God answers prayer! Paul knew it, and that's why he shared these requests.

Paul's Praise

Second, Paul praised the Lord for His faithfulness in meeting the needs of Christians. He wrote, "But the Lord is faithful, and he will strengthen and protect you from the evil one. We have confidence in the Lord that you are doing and will continue to do the things we command" (2 Thess. 3:3,4).

Paul was praising the Lord for His faithfulness in three areas. First, he praised Him for strengthening Christians, for making them firm and solid in their convictions concerning spiritual truth. The verb, "to make firm and solid" is in the future tense, indicating that this is a continuous thing God does for the believer.

Second, he praised Him for protecting the Christians from the evil one. The verb "to protect" is the Greek *philaxi;* it literally means, "to guard," "to defend," "to keep safe." This verb is also in the future tense, indicating that this is something God continues to do for His children.

Third, Paul praised the Lord for His faithfulness in motivating Christians to implement the commands of the Scripture in their lives. In this connection we need to bear in mind that the commands which Paul issued to the Thessalonians were not something that he made up; they were from the Lord.

There is one more important truth that we need to see in order to understand all that Paul is saying in these verses. That truth is related to the ministry of the Holy Spirit.

It is the Holy Spirit working in the life of the believer that enables him to be firm and solid in his convictions concerning spiritual truth. Without this ministry on his life he cannot even understand elementary spiritual concepts (see 1 Cor. 2:14).

It is the Holy Spirit who guards, defends and keeps safe every Christian when he is attacked by the evil one (the devil). This is why Paul commanded, "Do not grieve the Holy Spirit of God, with whom you were sealed for the day of redemption" (Eph. 4:30). Satan may gain a temporary victory in the life of the believer, but this he cannot do eternally. The Holy Spirit who constantly fights him in behalf of the Christian is God's guarantee that the Christian is kept safe in Christ Jesus. This is what being sealed by the Holy Spirit for the day of redemption means.

It is the Holy Spirit who motivates the Christian to implement the commands of the Scripture in his life. Jesus said in John 16:13, "When he, the Spirit of truth, comes, he will guide you into all truth." The more completely we yield ourselves to the Holy Spirit, the more effective we become in carrying out the directives of our Saviour.

Paul's Prayer

In 2 Thessalonians 3 verse 5 Paul prayed for his Thessalonian friends. Notice the words of that verse: "May the Lord direct your hearts into God's love and Christ's perseverance." Just a cursory reading of this reveals that Paul's prayer is twofold.

First, he prayed that the Lord would direct their hearts into the love of God. The implication of this is tremendous. Simply stated it is this: Paul was praying that God would make his brothers and sisters in Christ aware of the fact that they could not drift beyond His love and care. Regardless of the circumstances they faced—whether they be adverse or easy, whether they be hostile or friendly, whether they be sickness or health, prosperity or poverty—He would always be near them in love.

When I was a young preacher I called upon one of the leaders of our denomination who was recuperating from his third serious heart attack. He described some of the difficulties he had experienced. Then he said, "But the Lord was with me. I could sense His love. And I discovered what Moses meant when he wrote, 'The eternal God is thy refuge, and underneath are the everlasting arms'" (Deut. 33:27, *KJV*).

136

Second, because the Thessalonian Christians had a tendency to be anxious concerning the return of the Lord, even to the point of letting their imaginations run wild in this matter, Paul prayed that the Lord would direct their hearts into "Christ's perseverance." "Persevere" is a translation of the Greek noun *hupomona* which comes from the verb *hupomeno* which means "to bear up under," "to endure," "to continue firm," "to hold out," "to remain constant." Paul was praying that the Lord would lay it on the hearts of the Thessalonian Christians to persevere in their service to Him while waiting for His return.

And what Paul prayed for the Thessalonians at this point is God's will for every Christian. Jesus spelled this out during His post-resurrection ministry when He was asked by His disciples about the time He would establish His Kingdom. He answered, "It is not for you to know the times or dates the Father has set by his own authority. But you will receive power when the Holy Spirit comes on you; and you will be my witnesses in Jerusalem, and in all Judea and Samaria, and to the ends of the earth" (Acts 1:7,8). While we await the return of our Saviour, it is God's will that we should persevere in serving Him by sharing our faith with others. It is just that simple.

When W.E. Blackstone, author of the book, *Jesus Is Coming,* was asked if he was still looking for the Lord, he replied, "I'm looking for the Lord every day, but I'm hustling to get the chores done before He gets here." Are you doing the same?

Paul's Commendation

Following the section on the subject of undisciplined Christians (2 Thessalonians 3:6-15, discussed in chapter

11), Paul came to his closing words of the epistle.

In verses 16-18 Paul, as a father, commended the Thessalonian Christians as his spiritual children to the Lord Jesus Christ, who would deal with them on the basis of grace and give them peace. He writes, "Now may the Lord of peace himself give you peace at all times and in every way. The Lord be with all of you . . . . The grace of our Lord Jesus Christ be with you all."

As I read these verses one day a picture came to my mind. It was the picture of a father kneeling down and praying, commending his children into the hands of Jesus Christ. This he did because he knew the Lord would deal with them not on the basis of what they deserved, but on the basis of what they needed. This would result in their being at peace with God, with their fellow Christians, and with themselves.

Shortly after I "saw" this picture, I was talking to a fellow preacher. He was excited as he told me about his 17-year-old son who had been giving him trouble. He said, "Finally I realized that I couldn't do anything with him, even though I had given him the best of Christian training in the home. At this point I knelt down and commended him to the Saviour, and He took over. Shortly after that, my son went to a camp where the Holy Spirit really spoke to Him. Now he is on fire for God. He is witnessing to his faith, and he is once more a son to me in the truest sense of that word."

You see, the Lord dealt with that boy on the basis of grace and gave him peace.

And the Lord will do the same for you if you will commend yourself to Him; and He will do the same for your children, providing you will commend them to Him. He may not do it on your time schedule, but He will do it.

138

Bibliography

Barclay, William. *The Letters to the Philippians, Colossians and Thessalonians.* Edinburgh: The Saint Andrew Press, 1959.

Benson, David. *Miracle in Moscow.* Ventura: Regal Books, 1975.

Chafer, Lewis Sperry. *Systematic Theology.* Dallas: Dallas Seminary Press, 1948.

Denney, James. *The Epistle to the Thessalonians.* New York: A.C. Armstrong and Sons, 1903.

Gillquist, Peter. *Love Is Now.* Grand Rapids: Zondervan Publishing House, 1970.

Harris, Stephen P. *My Anchor Held.* Old Tappan: Fleming H. Revell Company, 1970.

Hiebert, Edmond. *The Thessalonian Epistles: A Call to Readiness.* Chicago: Moody Press, 1971.

Lindsay, Hal. *There's a New World Coming.* Irvine: Harvest House Publishers, 1973.

MacLaren, Alexander. *Expositions of Holy Scripture.* Grand Rapids: Baker Book House, 1974.

Schaeffer, Francis A. *Death in the City.* Downers Grove: Inter-Varsity Press, 1969.

Vine, W.E. *Expository Dictionary of New Testament Words.* Westwood: Fleming H. Revell Company, 1940.